What people are saying about

Pagan Portals - Loki

Dagulf Loptson provides a clear, well-supported and appealing introduction to Loki's character, history, and presence in the world. In addition to scholarship that will bolster your case if you find yourself defending him, Loptson provides ideas and directions for creating rituals and ritual gear. Loptson's work on Loki played a major part in my decision to reconsider my view on this often misunderstood god. The Trickster plays an important role in creating change, and we need his help today.

Diana Paxson, author of *Essential Ásatrú: Walking the Path of Northern Paganism*

Pagan Portals - Loki is a bold and necessary look at the Trickster God of the Norse. The author deftly weaves together academic material and personal experience to give the reader a guide not only to better understand this often maligned deity but also to connect directly to him. An unflinching appraisal that offers a great deal of insight into Loki.

Morgan Daimler, author of *Pagan Portals - Odin* and *Pagan Portals - Thor*

Pagan Portals
Loki

Trickster and Transformer

Pagan Portals
Loki

Trickster and Transformer

Dagulf Loptson

**MOON
BOOKS**

Winchester, UK
Washington, USA

JOHN HUNT PUBLISHING

First published by Moon Books, 2020
Moon Books is an imprint of John Hunt Publishing Ltd., No. 3 East Street, Alresford
Hampshire SO24 9EE, UK
office@jhpbooks.net
www.johnhuntpublishing.com
www.moon-books.net

For distributor details and how to order please visit the 'Ordering' section on our website.

Text copyright: Dagulf Loptson 2019

ISBN: 978 1 78904 309 9
978 1 78904 310 5 (ebook)
Library of Congress Control Number: 2019943879

A CIP catalogue record for this book is available from the British Library.

Design: Stuart Davies

Printed and bound by CPI Group (UK) Ltd, Croydon, CR0 4YY

We operate a distinctive and ethical publishing philosophy in
all areas of our business, from our global network of authors to
production and worldwide distribution.

Contents

This book is dedicated to Loki Laufeyjarson and those who love him. A special thank you to my wife Michelle for always being there to inspire and encourage me. Thank you to all of my spiritual teachers and guides: especially Jeff, who pointed the way to Agni.

Introduction - Who is Loki?

"That one is also reckoned among the Æsir whom some call the Æsir's calumniator and originator of deceits and the disgrace of all gods and men. His name is Loki or Lopt, son of the giant Farbauti. Laufey or Nal is his mother. Byleist and Helblindi are his brothers. Loki is pleasing and handsome in appearance, evil in character, very capricious in behavior. He possessed to a greater degree than others the kind of learning that is called cunning, and tricks for every purpose. He was always getting the Æsir into a complete fix and often got them out of it by trickery."[1]

Snorri Sturluson, Gylfaginning

Loki is one of the most famous, and at the same time, one of the most controversial deities in the Norse Pantheon. He is the great trickster of Norse Mythology: often getting the gods into trouble and then getting them out of it again. The picture that Snorri paints of him in his Edda is a conflicted one. On one hand, he is the father of monsters, the instigator of Baldr's death, and one of the key players at Ragnarök: the doom of the gods. At the same time, he is the sworn blood-brother of Óðinn, the favorite traveling companion of Þórr, and the source of the god's most important treasures. He is the husband of Sigyn, an Æsir goddess connected to themes of victory, and is the lover of Angrboða: a fearsome giantess who gives birth to a brood of werewolves in the Járnviðr ("iron wood"). He is the son of a Jötunn (often translated to "giant", but literally meaning "devourer") and an Ásyunjur (goddess), which has often made it uncertain whether he himself should be counted as a Jötunn or an Ás (god). His contradictory nature even extends to his gender, and as the master shapeshifter of Ásgarðr he is both the father and the mother of a number of magical beings. While there isn't sufficient evidence to prove whether or not he received cult worship in Scandinavia

1

and Western Europe, that doesn't stop him from dominating the action of Norse mythology: sometimes as a comic relief and ally of the gods, sometimes as their antagonist. He doesn't conform to the classical image of the noble, Viking warrior, often resorting to trickery and magic rather than brute force.

Loki's place in Old Norse cosmology isn't something that's easily defined, and he seems to defy every attempt to categorize him. Perhaps it's for this reason that he has been interpreted in so many different ways by so many different people. In the Pagan and Heathen communities, just the mention of his name is likely to bring up a variety of different reactions. Some people firmly believe him to be an enemy of the gods and persona non grata in their circles. Other people may view him as a less sinister clown or prankster: one whose jokes often got out of hand. There are still others who feel called to Loki as a god of non-conformity, transformation, and living by your wits. Those who are devoted to this often contradictory deity (as I am myself) experience him in many different ways: some see him as a teacher, a guide, a protector, a friend, or sometimes even a lover. Regardless of how you see him, he's a force that burns brightly in the Norse Myths and he's impossible to ignore.

Loki came into my life at a young age in 1994, and ever since then he has been at the center of my devotional life. Through most of my life's important lessons he has been there to teach and to guide (and sometimes roll his eyes). My vision of him has expanded and grown over the years, and the master shapeshifter wears many masks. He is the teller of unpleasant truths, the breaker of the bonds, the fire born from lightning that changes everything it touches. He is the challenger of authority and the disrupter of stagnation. To those that choose (or more correctly, are chosen) to walk the road of his mysteries, he is an uncompromising mirror that causes us to confront our true natures... with the understanding that self-knowledge is the source of all true power. He's here to kick the soapbox out from under our feet when we get consumed by illusions of grandeur, and he's here to lift us up into the light when we diminish our own self-worth. He's there to laugh knowingly when we fall into our own traps (as he so often does himself), but is there to help us transform our folly into wisdom. For many Lokeans (a word to describe those who claim Loki as their patron deity) he is a compass that always points inward, towards the light of personal sovereignty. He is a fire that will consume you, transform you, and inspire you. He will teach you to break the rules, live authentically, and never apologize for who you are. Like the trickster himself, by walking his path he will teach you his own virtues of self-sufficiency, self-acceptance, creative problem solving, and marching to the beat of your own drum.

If you have picked up this book, I assume that you are at least nominally interested in Loki or in building a devotional relationship with him. While we don't know if Loki ever received devotional worship in quite the same way other gods did in ancient Scandinavia that should be no obstacle to those who feel a call to worship him in modern times. It may be that Loki was always a god for the individual and those (who like Loki himself) stood a little outside the norms of society. It may be that Loki has been a part of your life for years, or you may just be getting to know him. Whatever the case, this book is intended to be an exploration of the many different facets of Loki's character as I have come to know him. Each chapter will focus on one of Loki's myths, one of his primary *heiti* (poetic bynames) from the Eddas, and will include a devotional or magical action to work with him. By the end of this book you will have everything you need to have a functional, devotional practice with Loki. Loki isn't a god you can really know by just reading his stories or what other people have written about him: he's a deity that needs to be experienced. For that reason, if you want to deepen your knowledge of Loki I encourage you not just to read through this book, but to work through it. Dedicating one week to each chapter and getting a chance to immerse yourself in the energies of his different aspects will give him the chance to teach you who he is by showing you. This book is a roadmap, but Loki is the real teacher.

A Warning

Those who shun Loki aren't necessarily afraid of him for no reason. Loki is a trickster and an agent of change, which can be unpredictable and terrifying. The transformation he brings may be internal or external, and in calling Loki's presence into your life you may lose parts of yourself along the way that you thought were vital and important. However, Loki's tricks always serve a purpose, and if his challenges are met with bravery instead of fear we may find ourselves becoming something greater than we were before. Before you get in too deep, now is the time to ask yourself: am I ready for change?

With all of that said, I hope you enjoy this humble attempt to introduce you to the god who rules my heart.

Hail Loki!

Sources for Loki's Myths

The oldest known Skaldic poem to mention Loki was written by Þjóðólf of Hvin, who was the contemporary of the Norwegian king Harald Finehair (who died in 945). This was in the poem *Haustlöng* ("autumn-long"), which Snorri Sturluson preserved in his poetry manual *Skaldskaparmál*[2]. There is large variety of other literature in which Loki's stories are preserved, and I will be referring to many of them in this book. For those who are unfamiliar with Old Norse myth and literature, I'm including this list of sources for your own reference and future research. It's noteworthy that many of these myths were recorded hundreds of years after the conversion of Scandinavia, (taking place between the 8th and 12th centuries, with Iceland officially converting in 1000 CE) and it's therefore uncertain how much of

Loki's character and mythos was influenced by the introduction of a worldview with a dualistic vision of morality. Trickster figures like Loki are often difficult to compartmentalize in paradigms that depend on an absolute good and absolute evil, and they often are presented through a sinister lens by Christian commentators. I am personally of the opinion that Loki's character was not originally as maligned as it became, and as a sacred trickster he is a deity that straddles the lines of morality and social norms. I therefore caution you to consider the sources of these materials and reach your own conclusions.

The Elder Edda: This Edda is a collection of mythic and heroic poems that were recorded in Iceland around 1270, and it is properly known as the *Codex Regius* ("Royal Book"). While this book is a source of mythology, it doesn't necessarily reflect any Scandinavian religious tradition, and rather was composed for its poetic and historical value. Even so, some hints towards religious belief can be gleaned from it, and it contains many stories about Loki. There are many available translations of the Elder Edda, though I recommend looking for modern translations made by credible scholars such as Andy Orchard, Carolyne Larrington, and Jackson Crawford.

The Prose Edda: This Edda was written by the Icelandic politician and poet Snorri Sturluson, who was born in 1179 and killed in 1241. It is written in two parts: *Gylfaginning* ("The Tricking of Gylfi"), and *Skáldskaparmál* ("The Language of Poetry"). Though Snorri was a Christian author, he was very interested in the poetry and myths of his ancestors, and compiled his Edda in an effort to teach and restore the fading art of Skaldic Poetry. Many of the famous myths of the gods (including Loki) come to us from Snorri, though like the *Codex Regius*, Snorri's Edda is not a manual of Scandinavian paganism. Snorri received clerical training in his youth (though he didn't become a priest). He was acquainted with Greek mythology (explaining in his prologue how the Æsir were actually Trojan magicians, not gods), and was most likely working from surviving poems in his possession and Icelandic oral tradition. It is likely that all of these elements influenced Snorri's reshaping and retelling of these stories, though they are beautifully written and very accessible. I recommend the translation by Anthony Faulkes.

Gesta Danorum ("The Deeds of the Danes"): This is the first great, Danish history, written in the between 1185 and 1222 by the historian and theologian Saxo Grammaticus. Saxo's work is composed of 16 volumes that chart the history of Denmark from a mythical pre-history to the late 12th century. A figure who might be the equivalent of Snorri's Loki (called "Utgarthilocus by Saxo) appears in part two of book eight. Utgarthilocus (Útgarðr Loki) appears in a position much like Loki himself does in Snorri's Edda and the Eddic poem *Lokasenna*: bound in a cave and surrounded by poisonous snakes. Interestingly, Utgarthilocus is also described as the focus of worship for a Danish king named Gorm the Old. I recommend the translation by Hilda Ellis Davidson.

Völsunga saga (The Saga of the Völsungs): This saga was recorded during the latter part of the 13th century, and chronicles the history of the Völsung family. This saga begins with a story about how Loki stole a golden treasure and a cursed ring from a dwarf named Andvari in order to repay the death of Otr (who he killed while Otr was in the form of an otter). The ring plays a large role in the story that ensues, which was the primary inspiration for Richard Wagner's famous Ring Cycle operas as well as The Lord of the Rings by J.R.R Tolkien. I recommend the translation by Jesse Byock.

Sörla þattr (Sörli's Tale): This is a short narrative appearing in the *Flateyjarbók* ("Flat Island Book"): an Icelandic collection of sagas that was completed around 1394. . It preserves a story about how Óðinn commissioned Loki to steal Freyja's famous Brísingamen necklace for him.

Lokka Táttur (Loki's Tale): This is a ballad from the Faroe

Islands that was first recorded in the late 18th century, but probably dates back to the Middle Ages[3]. It contains a story in which Loki helps to rescue a little boy from a giant.

Loke in the Younger Tradition: This is an article by the Danish folklorist Axel Olrik, first appearing in the publication Særtryk Af Danske Sudier in 1909. In it are a variety of surviving folk-sayings and tales relating to Loki that he collected from many different parts of Scandinavia.

Chapter 1

Loptr: The Fire from Heaven

Let me tell you a story, which might be true...

Loki's mother was an Ásynjur named Laufey, which means "leafy": a kenning for a tree. His father was a Jötunn named Fárbauti, which means "cruel striker". When the world was dark and the earth was new, Fárbauti fell from heaven in the form of lightning, and struck Loki´s mother, who is also called Nál or "needle", because she herself was tall and thin. She may have been a slender, white, birch, which those who are wise in Runes know as the "leafiest of trees". When Fárbauti struck her, she burst into flame: giving birth to their son, Loki. The ancestors saw that this fire was born from the union of heaven and earth, and knew that it was no ordinary fire: it was one of holy origin, sent from the sky by the gods. This fire had the power to take messages and gifts back to the heavens where it came from through rites of holy sacrifice. It had the power to burn witches and draugr and drive away evil spirits. Óðinn himself saw the value in such an ally, and named Loki as his sworn blood-brother. He would not accept a drink if Loki was not offered a drink too... and indeed, none of the gods drink unless it is carried to them through the ritual of sacrifice. But like all fire, this fire from heaven also had its capricious side. Fire is its own master, and will burn his friends as easily as he'll burn his enemies if he's not handled carefully. He is born with the power to enliven and create, but also holds the power to destroy. But just as fire may burn the dead overgrowth of a forest, it also leaves the potential for healing and new growth in its wake.

Though Loki is undeniably one of the most important players in Norse Mythology, he is one whose origins are largely shrouded in mystery. Though Snorri calls him handsome in *Gylfaginning,* the master shapeshifter is otherwise never physically described. His name is typically attributed to the word *loka* in Old Norse, which means to "lock" or "close". Even his name immediately presents us with a mystery. What does Loki close? Does this refer to the closure he brings to the world at Ragnarök? Does it refer to the deals he closes in more than one story? If he closes, is he also the god who opens? Loki's name has also been tied to the southern Swedish word *locke*, meaning "spider" by Anna Birgitta Rooth[4]. This is an interesting theory, considering that Loki himself was described by Snorri as the inverter of the fishnet and the mother of an eight-legged horse in *Gylfaginning*. Loki as the spider may be seen as a weaver of nets, but perhaps also as a weaver of fate.

We don't know for sure how or when Loki became associated with the Æsir (the family of deities that live in Ásgarðr), though he himself is listed as an Æsir and described as an Ás by Snorri Sturluson. He is also called an Ás in many of his own bynames and kennings. His mother Laufey is listed among the Ásynjur (goddesses) by Snorri, which may explain why Loki is known by the atypical maternal surname of Laufeyjarson ("son of Laufey"), as his mother's rank would have been considered higher than his Jötunn father's. It may also be that Laufey was a giantess who came to be counted among the Æsir, just like Freyr's wife Gerðr or Njorðr's wife Skaði were, but if that is the case there's no surviving literature to support such a story. I personally consider Laufey to be a birch goddess much like the Germanic goddesses Holda and Birchta, because the Birch rune poems describe the birch as being a leafy tree (Laufey's name means "leafy), and the Norwegian rune poem for *Bjarkan* is the only rune poem in which Loki's name appears, possibly linking Loki to the birch tree:

(Birch-twig) is the limb greenest with leaves;
Loki brought the luck of deceit[5]

9

According to Snorri, Loki has two brothers who he calls Býleistr (possibly meaning "wind and lighting") and Helblindi ("Hel blind"). These two figures are only found in kennings for Loki where he is referred to as either "Brother of Býleistr" or "Brother of Helblindi". As both of these names seem to be *heiti* of Óðinn's (Óðinn being Loki's blood-brother according to *Lokasenna*), it may be that Snorri inferred a separate identity for these two names when in fact there was none.

One of Loki's common bynames in Skaldic and Eddic poetry was Loptr, which has been translated as "lofty one" or one who is "aloft". There are multiple stories where Loki borrows the falcon skin cloak of either Freyja or Frigg in order to perform some kind of mission for the gods, and this name could point to Loki's ability to travel through the air. In a slightly more mysterious bit of lore, Snorri tells us that Loki was also the possessor of a pair of shoes which allowed him to walk through the air and over water, much like the Greek Hermes. Another possible interpretation for Loptr is that it is a derivation from *lopt-eldr,* which translates to "sky fire", or "lightning" in Old Norse[6]. This *heiti* may point back to Loki's father Fárbauti, the "cruel striker", whom many have interpreted to be symbolic of a lightning strike. Loki as the lightning that travels through the sky with his frequent traveling companion Þórr ("thunder") is also a compelling interpretation.

Much as this byname suggests, Loki's energy can be experienced like a lightning strike. He has a great deal in common with another Indo-European enlightenment bringer, Prometheus, who steals fire from the gods for humanity. Loki is able to use his wit and think outside the box to resolve many of the god's problems (even if they are ones he himself created). He has the potential to bring this same clarity and quickness of thought to those who count him as a friend. Loki is tricky, and we can easily be deceived by the shadows that the light casts. However, light can also cut through deception and show us the world as it really is. Paradoxically, Loki is called *frumkveða flærðanna* ("father of lies") by Snorri. Whether or not this was attempt to link him to Lucifer (another "light bringer") in his Christian audience's minds is uncertain. The Kirkby Stephen Stone (A fragmented, 10th century cross in St. Stephen's Church, England) depicts a horned, bound figure which has either been interpreted as an image of Loki or as an image of Lucifer imprisoned at the end of the world. This could point to a gradual conflation of the two images as Western Europe gradually become Christianized. What is apparent from Loki's stories is that he more often got in trouble for telling the truth than for deception.

Creating a Loki Candle

Though Loki is never explicitly named as a "fire deity" in any of our surviving sources for him, he is so often connected to fire and themes of fire in his stories and folklore that many Lokeans have fully embraced his interpretation as a fire god. I personally relate to the gods as the sentient souls behind the forces of nature, and therefore I believe that any sacred fire which is lit with intention can literally become the body of Loki and a vehicle through which we in Midgarðr (the world of humans) can connect to him. Therefore, as a first step in your Lokean journey I'm presenting you with a way to create and consecrate a ritual candle towards building a devotional practice with Loki. There are no specific colors that are traditionally associated with Loki, but if you would like to choose an appropriate color for your candle, here is a list that I personally associate with him:

Loki Color Associations:
   Orange, Red, Gold, Yellow, Black, Green, Violet

What you will need:
   1 large, orange pillar candle in a color of your choice
   1 tool to inscribe the candle, such as a nail
   Matches or a lighter
   1 Lancet

(Blood magic is a tool that is often used in Scandinavian folk magic to empower staves and magical items. I will recommend its use more than once in this book. If you are going to be using a lancet to draw blood from your finger, make sure to sterilize the area with alcohol first and dispose of any sharps safely. If you aren't comfortable or able to use blood, spit is another magically loaded substance. Mixing red ochre powder with linseed oil can also serve as a substitute for blood, as it resembles the color of life.)

   When you have gathered your items, you will first carve a

bind rune into the candle. A bind rune is a pictograph which is created through the combination of multiple runes, often to express a word, a name, or to act as a magical sigil. In this case, the bind rune is made up of the runes of the Elder Futhark and is representative of Loki's name, which is an extension of his power. As you carve, you may feel compelled to improvise a prayer or petition to Loki to bless the candle and make it a vehicle through which you can commune with him and he can enter our world.

When you have finished carving the stave, use the lancet to get a drop of blood from one of your fingers and dab it onto the symbol. Adding blood to the stave will activate it and give it life. If you desire, you can either chant Loki's name or the runes of the Elder Futhark which make up his name: Laguz, Othala, Kenaz, and Isa.

When the candle has been activated, place it in front of you, and say this prayer while you light it, bowing slightly to the candle after it is lit:

I light the flame of Loki, both without me and within me

With your candle lit, sit for a while and stare at the flame. Sit in Loki's presence and observe what you feel. As you breathe in, imagine that through your breath you are being filled with the light of your candle. This light transforming into golden fire inside of your body. The flames dance within you, burning away any fears, blockages, or emotional turmoil. Feel Loki's warmth and inspiration spread throughout you. You can continue this fire breathing as long as you like. Use this as an opportunity to begin a dialog with Loki. What does his energy feel like? Does he have any messages for you? Do you have anything you want to say to him?

Chapter 2

Vé: The Holy Enclosure

Many years ago, when the gods had just established the world and built Valhöll, a smith appeared in Ásgarðr and claimed that he could build them a massive wall within three seasons that would protect them from the giants. In exchange for his work he asked for the sun, the moon, and the goddess Freyja as his bride. The gods held a council and came up with a cunning plan. They stipulated that they would only pay the price if he was able to build the entire wall, by himself, in only one winter. If any part of the wall remained unfinished by summer, then his payment would be forfeit. The smith agreed to their impossible terms, but only if he was allowed to use his stallion named Svaðilfari to help him work. The gods were suspicious, but it was Loki who finally talked them into letting the smith use his horse. The gods made a deal with the smith, invoking witnesses and holy oaths that they would keep their end of the bargain.

On the first day of winter the smith began his work, and the gods were very alarmed to see that the horse Svaðilfari was able to haul enormous pieces of stone from the quarry to the wall almost effortlessly. The wall was going up with amazing speed, and when there were only three days left until the beginning of summer, the smith had nearly finished his work. The gods came together in council, and demanded from one another whose bright idea it had been to allow the smith to use his horse. They unanimously came to the conclusion that it must have been Loki's fault, and they threatened him within an inch of his life if he couldn't come up with a way to save Freyja, the sun, and the moon. Afraid of the violence the gods were threatening, Loki made an oath that he would find a way to stop the smith at any cost.

That evening, as the smith and Svaðilfari were hard at work, a mare suddenly appeared out of the forest and whinnied at the stallion. Svaðilfari was mad with excitement, and broke his reigns and went chasing after the mare. The smith tried to catch the two horses, but they evaded him and ran off together through the forest all night. By the next morning no more work had been done, and without his horse the smith's progress slowed to a crawl. When he realized that he was about to be cheated out of all of his hard work, the smith flew into a rage, and revealed himself to be one of the Jötnar. When the gods realized what he was, they disregarded their oaths and Þórr slew him with his hammer. Months later, Loki surprisingly gave birth to a foal, as he had shape-shifted himself into the mare to lure Svaðilfari away from his work. The foal's unusual parentage assured that he would be no ordinary horse. He was grey and had eight legs, and could travel anywhere and slip into any corner of 9 worlds. For this reason he was called Sleipnir ("the slipper"), and was given to Óðinn as his steed. Thus it was through trickery that Loki secured a sacred enclosure around Asgarðr.

There are two accounts of the creation of humans in Eddic literature: one in the poem *Völuspá* and the other in Snorri's *Gylfaginning*. In the *Völuspá* account, humans are created out of two fallen trees by a triad of gods: Óðinn, Hænir, and an otherwise unknown deity named Lóðurr (possibly another name of Loki's). In Snorri's Edda and in his book of Norwegian history, *Heimskringla*, he replaces two of these creative deities with the names Vili and Vé. Vili and Vé are another pair of mysterious figures, and have been interpreted as two aspects of Óðinn, two alternate names for Hænir and Lóðurr, or as two entirely independent deities. I personally have adopted the idea that Vili ("will") is an alternate name for the god Hænir, who seems to be connected to the idea of the *hugr*: one's personal mind and will. That leaves Vé as an alternate name of Lóðurr/Loki.

The name Vé has sometimes been translated as "holiness", but a *vé* is also a noun, meaning a holy space, temple, or sanctuary.

The word is derived from the Germanic word *wīhaz* meaning "sacred" or "holy"[7]. There is a surviving hint of how holy spaces such as these might have been consecrated and set apart in *Landnámabók*, which is a medieval Icelandic text that chronicles the settling and history of early Iceland:

> *"A three-cornered plot of land lay unappropriated to the east of the Fleet, between Cross-river and Jalda-stone. This plot of land Jorund went round by fire and set it aside for a temple."*[8]

This act of "land taking" by walking around a piece of land with fire occurs more than once in *Landnámabók*. Just as fire was believed to have a purifying effect on dark forces in the Eddas in Sagas, so it seems that it also has a sanctifying effect here. In a roundabout way, just as fire seems to have been used towards the sanctification of holy places, so too does Loki bring about the creation of a boundary of protection around Ásgarðr.. The idea that the gods must be shielded from unclean forces through some kind of barrier or boundary is also echoed in the function of the *vé-bönd*, which were a type of band that were fastened to stakes and would form the boundaries of a shrine or other sacred place. If Loki and Vé are indeed one in the same, Loki's role as the obtainer of Ásgarðr's wall becomes that much more significant.

Though Loki does not have the reputation of a fighter or defender in the way that deities like Óðinn, Þórr, or even Freyja do, if we view him through the lens of a god of sacred fire, it is only logical that those devoted to him would be able to call upon his aspect as Vé to sanctify their own holy spaces. There are a variety of reasons that one may choose to sanctify a space such as this to do their own worship or spiritual work. Cleansing a space helps to neutralize it of any malignant spirits or spiritual miasma that may take a harmful toll on a devotee through either spiritual, mental, or physical means. It is also good practice to cleanse any space in which a god or other holy being will be called upon and worshiped: just like it's polite to clean your house before inviting a guest over. A common method of sanctification that is found in many cultures across the world is through fumigating a space by burning sacred plants and by carrying fire through or around it.

Making Lokean Recels and Performing a Cleansing

"Recels" is the Old English word for incense, which as they are today were believed to have healing and purifying abilities. To create your own recels, you will combine a mixture of dry herbs together. Once the herbs are gathered, they are easiest to burn by grinding them down with a mortar and pestle, then burning them on a charcoal disc in a safe container. Burn the disk on either a pile of sand or salt to dispense the heat. Though with the exception of dandelion there aren't any plants in this list that hold any historical connection to Loki, these are ingredients that I personally associate with him. According to Axel Olrik, dandelions were called Låkkilæjerin ("Loki blooms") in Jutland[9].

Loki Herb Associations:

Dandelion, Mullein, Dragon's Blood Resin, Cinnamon, Star Anise, Mistletoe, Clove

What you will need:

Your Loki Pillar Candle

Your Lokean Recels and a container for them

1 charcoal disc

Matches or a lighter

(Optional) Feathers or a fan to direct the smoke with

To cleanse your space, first light your Loki candle, carrying it around the perimeter of the area, repeating this prayer like a mantra as you do so:

Eldr brenna. (Eld-er bren-ah)
Eldr hreinsa. (Eld-er Hrayn-sah)
Eldr Loka. (Elder-er Low-kah)
Eyddi skugga (Ay-dee Skoo-gah)

Fire burn,
Fire purify,
Loki's fire
Dispel shadow

Next, light your charcoal and sprinkle some of your recels on it to create smoke. Carry the smoke throughout the space, using your hand, feathers, or fan to direct the smoke into all four directions. Continue your prayer as you do so. If the smoke is thick and you're inside, don't forget to open a window or door. The candle and recels can also be used to cleanse yourself by moving the lit candle carefully around your body and fumigating yourself with the smoke from the top of your head to the bottom of your feet.

Chapter 3

Lóðurr: The Life Giver

Not long after the world had been created, Óðinn, Hænir, and Lóðurr were traveling together, as they often still do. They were walking along the newly formed earth when they stumbled upon two trees: an ash and an elm. Seeing that the trees were incapable of much and had no destinies, the gods decided to make them a little more interesting. They carved faces into the wood, and each god gave the trees a gift. Óðinn gave them önd, the breath of life. Hænir gave them óðr, consciousness and will. Finally, Lóðurr gave them lá and litu góða, blood and the color of life. The trees were now sentient, and could move, think, and act with their own will, setting their destinies into motion. The ash tree became Askr, the first man. The elm became Embla, the first woman.

Just as the gods formed humans from two trees, so would humans ever afterwards form bodies for the gods in similar ways. The ancestors carved images of the gods from trees, then they would name them, give them purpose, give them adornments, and most importantly, give them blood to strengthen them. Just as the gods shaped man, so has man shaped the gods.

Lóðurr is a very little known deity, but due to his only appearance with Óðinn and Hænir in the Eddic poem *Völuspá*, some scholars have speculated that Lóðurr may be an alternate name of Loki's. Loki is the only other deity who often appears with Óðinn and Hænir in a triad, and he appears together with them in the Skaldic poem *Haustlöng*, in the Eddic poem *Reginsmál*, in *Völsungasaga* (the Saga of the Völsungs), In Snorri's *Skáldskaparmál*, and in the Faroese ballad *Lokka Táttur*. In Haustlöng, Loki is referred to by the kennings *Hrafn-ásar vinr* ("the raven-god's, i.e. Óðinn's friend", and *Hænirs vinr* (Hænir's friend"). The addition of Loki in this triad in every poem except for *Völuspá* could mean that Loki is actually an abbreviation or pet-name for Lóðurr[10].

Though because of its late date it's uncertain whether or not it is preserving an ancient tradition, Loki is directly referred to by the name Lóðurr in the Icelandic ballad called *Þrymlur*, thought to be written between1300-1400 CE. Þrymlur is a retelling of the Eddic poem *Þrymskviða* written in rímur meters (one of the many styles of Icelandic poetry). In the poem, Loki is greeted by the giant Þrym:

> 21. *The ugly one speaks in a cunning way –*
> *he inquired in smooth words –*
> *Lóður come you hither in health,*
> *What call do yo have in inquiry?*[11]

Though it's uncertain whether or not Loki was identified with Lóðurr in antiquity, Haukur Þorgeirsson suggests that the author of Þrymlur may have known that Lóðurr was an alternate name of Loki's through Icelandic oral tradition[12].

Loki's name has also been potentially linked to Lóðurr's through an archeological find from Nordendorf, Germany. A safety-pin style brooch was found there that dates back to about the sixth century. There is a runic text scratched onto the back of the decorated part of the brooch, which might be calling upon three deities as part of a love amulet, or alternately has been interpreted as a Christian prayer denouncing the three gods:

Logaþore,
Wodan,
wigi Þonar.
Awa Leubwinii

The names "Wodan" and "wigi-Þonar" are recognizable as Óðinn and "blessing" Þórr. Logaþore seems to be the Old

German equivalent of the Old Norse Lóðurr, making a triad of three gods like the one found in Icelandic literature. Logaþore literally translates to "trickster" or "sorcerer", so this could easily be considered either a proper name or a byname for Loki[13]. Regardless of the intention of the brooch itself, this could be an early, Germanic piece of evidence of Loki being included among other deities whose worship has been better and more clearly recorded.

Loki in the role of Lóðurr reveals his qualities as a creator god, which are often an aspect of his character that is overlooked. The tricksters of many other cultures often take the role of creators of the world, creators of men, and bringers of culture, which Loki himself provides in more than one instance. As the giver of blood, I also interpret Loki as a god who is linked to the spark of life and vitality in living creatures, who can be called upon to tap into our own creative qualities as artists, magicians, organizers, parents, or any other capacity.

Creating a Logaþore Amulet

The purpose of this amulet is to create a link to Loki and to utilize the creative powers of Lóðurr in constructing a living, magical object. In Scandinavian magic, staves are often carved into significant objects, given an intention, have words spoken over them, and are awakened with some type of blood or other substance. This creative action closely resembles the process through which Askr and Embla were first created by the gods, who themselves were filled with breath, will, and blood.

You'll want to choose an amulet that you can wear around your neck, either by adding a hole for a cord in a piece of wood or metal or buying something pre-made.

What you will need:
Your Loki candle
Lokean recels

A piece of wood or metal that can be turned into a pendant
A cord or chain for the pendant
A lancet (blood can be substituted with red ochre or spit)
A dremel or wood-burner

To begin, light your Loki candle and recels and cleanse the amulet you've chosen by running it over the flame and through the smoke. You might use the cleansing chant you learned in the last chapter. When you've cleaned the amulet, carve, burn, or otherwise inscribe the name Logaþore into the amulet in Elder Futhark runes:

As you carve, you might choose to chant the names of the runes you're carving: Laguz, Othala, Gebo, Ansuz, Thurisaz, Othala, Raido, and Ehwaz. Otherwise, you can say a spontaneous prayer to Loki. Ask him to bless the amulet that it can be used as a connection to him and to you own powers of creativity. Breathe your prayer over the amulet so that like Askr and Embla it's filled with the breath of life. When the image has been carved, use the lancet to get a drop of blood from your finger, and awaken the runes by dabbing them with your blood. As you give the runes blood, say something to the effect of:

Logaþore, Logaþore, Logaþore I call you
Loki, Lóðurr, Loptr fill these staves with your might
By blood I awaken the holy runes
By blood I awaken the bond between us
May your inspiration burn within me now and always
Hail Loki

After the amulet has been created, it can be worn any time you wish to draw closer to Loki, when you are about to undergo any creative endeavor, or simply as a sign of devotion.

Chapter 4

In Slægi Áss: The Cunning God

Þórr's wife Sif was famous throughout the 9 worlds for her long, beautiful hair as golden as the wheat harvest. One morning, she awoke to find that every hair on her head had been completely cropped off, and she knew who the culprit was. Whether he had snuck into Sif's bedroom or had been invited, nobody knows, but one thing was for sure: Loki was to blame. When Þórr found Loki he threatened to break every bone in his body unless Loki was able to get Sif new hair, forged from gold by the dwarves. Loki went to a company of dwarves who were known as the sons of Ivaldi, and they created magical hair from gold that would grow on Sif's head just like real hair. They also created a magical ship called Skíðblaðnir for Freyr, and a spear called Gungnir for Óðinn that never misses its mark. But Loki can't quit while he's ahead. He also made a wager with another dwarf named Brokk that Brokk and his brother Eitri wouldn't be able to create three treasures that were as good as the ones make by Ivaldi's sons. Each of them was so confident that they bet their heads on it. Brokk and Eitri went to work, with Brokk blowing the bellows and Eitri shaping the metal. Together they created the golden boar named Gullinbursti for Freyr, an arm ring named Draupnir for Óðinn that made eight more of itself every 9th night, and a hammer called Mjölnir for Þórr. But the whole time they were working, a suspicious looking fly with a nasty bite continued to harass Brokk as if it were trying to impede his work. It's for this reason that Mjölnir has a short handle: because the fly bit Brokk so hard blood flowed into his eyes and he stopped pumping the bellows for just a moment. Of course, the fly had been Loki all along.

With the work done, Brokk and Loki brought their gifts to Ásgarðr so that the gods could judge between them. Though all of the work was amazing, the gods judged Mjölnir to be the greatest of the treasures, since with it Þórr would be able to protect the gods from all of their foes. When Loki realized he had lost the bet, he tried to escape with his magical shoes that could run over sky and sea. However, Þórr caught him and brought him back. Thinking quickly, Loki told Brokk that he could have his head, just as long as he didn't harm any part of his neck, as that hadn't been part of the wager. Since Brokk couldn't cut off Loki's head, he sewed his lips together instead, silencing him for at least a little while.

Like many of the trickster deities of other cultures, Loki is paradoxically both a bringer of chaos and a restorer of order. In many of his stories, his actions create conflict which has to be resolved (often by Loki himself) which leads to the gods receiving gifts or benefits that they didn't have before. The story of how Loki stole Sif's hair holds many layers of possible interpretation. Some have interpreted Sif's hair as symbolic of a wheat field, perhaps signifying that Sif was an agricultural goddess and a fitting partner for a god of storms and rain. In this interpretation, Loki has been imagined to represent a fire burning through the crops. Another possibility may be that Loki was poking fun at Sif's lack of fidelity, as cutting off the hair of an adulterous woman was a punishment implemented by the Germanic tribes according to the Roman historian Tacitus[14].

Loki's role in the creation of the god's greatest weapons and treasures is filled with more interesting implications. Out of all of the deities in the Norse Pantheon, Loki seems to have the closest relationship to a group of spiritual beings alternately known as the *svartálfar* ("dark elves") or *dvergar* ("dwarves"), who often appear in the myths as blacksmiths and craftsmen that specialize in making magical items. With Loki's many implied connections to fire, it may be that his role as a fire deity would have made him the natural ally of blacksmiths in the form of the fire of the forge. His connection to the forge has been further implied by an archeological find discovered on a beach in Snaptun, Denmark. This find was a stone tuyére: a tuyére being a tube or pipe through which air is blown into a forge in order to get the fire hot enough to melt metals while also shielding the bellows. This soapstone bellows-guard has been connected to Loki because of the image of a mustached face carved into it with a series of gashes across its mouth that have been interpreted as sewn lips. It may be that Loki's presence was being invoked in the forge because of his fiery nature. It has also been suggested that Loki's lips were sewn shut in order to protect the secrets of the blacksmith trade, since Loki had witnessed them while watching the dwarves in the shape of a fly. This could make image on the tuyére a not so subtle warning to outsiders to the craft who might spread their knowledge too readily.

In 2015, an amateur archeologist named Bent Hasen discovered an amulet from the Viking Age in Vejen, Denmark. As the image has markings over its mouth that resemble stitching, some have speculated that like the Snaptun Stone, it is also a representation of Loki[15].

Whether or not this amulet or even the Snaptun Stone were intended to be images of Loki can't be definitively proven, but that hasn't stopped modern Lokeans from finding inspiration in these images and adopting them for ourselves.

Blacksmithing was an art that was held in near-supernatural esteem throughout many parts of ancient Europe, often viewed as magical art as well as an artistic one. It therefore seems appropriate that Loki, himself a powerful magician and shapeshifter, should be associated with this transformative craft. Modern devotees have often pointed to this story in particular as one which reveals Loki's connection to craftsmanship and ability to inspire creativity in others.

Creating a Snaptun Stone

It is apparent through both archeological finds and later descriptions of Old Norse religion that the ancient Scandinavians and Germans created statues and other images of the gods as part of their worship. Though the Snaptun Stone was an object that had a functional purpose, we will be using it as inspiration to create a cult image for your devotional practice with Loki. Cult images are manmade images of the gods which are venerated, given offerings, and treated with respect as they represent the deity's presence on earth. While a sacred fire alone can be venerated as a literal manifestation of Loki, having a tangible, physical image is another useful link to his presence that offers him a more permanent anchor in your life.

While I can provide you guidelines on how to create this image, ultimately the creative process is up to you. You can use clay to make the "stone" and carve Loki's face into it while it's either wet or dry. You can also dremel or paint his face into a real stone. When I wanted to create my own cult image for Loki, I used an Icelandic lava rock. I made a small, cloth packet filled with natural objects that I find relevant to Loki's energies, then covered this and part of the stone with clay that I painted to blend in with the rest of the stone. When it had dried, I carved Loki's face into the clay and painted the inside of the image. You might also choose to imbue your stone with items you find relevant to Loki: dried plants, animal curios, gemstones, bones, ashes, or anything else that's meaningful to you. These can be burned into powder and mixed with your clay or paint, wrapped in a packet and hidden under rock or clay (as I did) or even packed and sealed into a hole in your stone. I would suggest you follow your own inspiration. I'm including a list of animal and stone associations that you can refer to while choosing your ingredients. With the exception of the fox (who some use as a modern symbol of Loki) the animals in this list are significant to him through his bynames, Scandinavian folklore, or animals he transforms into or is influenced by in the Eddas. The stones are my own inspiration, so use them as you see fit.

Loki Animal Associations:
Snake, spider, salmon, fox, fly, flea, seal, mare, vulture, falcon, wolf

Loki Stone Associations:
Carnelian, lava rock, obsidian, black onyx, garnet, citrine, serpentine

What you will need:
Your Loki image
Your Loki candle
Lokean recels   ·
1 lancet or blood substitute
An offering of your choice

After performing your cleansing ceremony in the space you'll be using, take your newly created image and pass it over your recel smoke and the flame of your candle to purify and energize it. To awaken your image, use your lancet to draw a drop of blood from your finger, and dab it onto your image (or do the same with your substitute). As you do so, say something to the effect of:

> *By fire, by breath, by blood I call you*
> *Loki Laufeyjarson*
> *By fire, by breath, by blood I call you*
> *As you crafted a body for Askr and Embla*
> *So too have I crafted a body for you*
> *To use as long as you desire*
> *Hail Loki*

As you finish your prayer, practice your fire breathing. Breathe the flame of your Loki candle into your lungs as you visualized before. As you exhale, imagine that you are passing Loki's fire into your image through your breathe. See it glowing with life in your mind's eye. It would now be appropriate to give an offering to Loki: whether a drink, food item, or something else. It would also be appropriate to choose a space to keep your image where it will be safe, whether that be an altar, a nightstand, or somewhere it can receive attention. You have created a living vessel for Loki, and therefore it must now be treated with the respect of a living thing. It isn't just a nicknack you can leave around the house to collect dust. Wash him when he's dusty, rub him with scented oils, give him offerings and candles now and then (or when you feel he wants something specific). Cult images are tools we can use to physically interact with and serve our deities as honored guests in our homes.

At this point, choosing an altar space to keep the sacred objects you are creating together in one place isn't a bad idea. I would recommend using your cleansing ritual to purify whichever space you intend to use before you install an altar for Loki there.

A Note about Offerings

Food and drink offerings are ways of sharing both energy and affection with our deities, just as you might offer a guest in your house something to eat if they came to visit you. As a rule of thumb, I don't offer my gods or spirits something I would be unwilling to put in my own mouth: if the offering is rotten, spoiled, or just not good, don't give it to them. I usually will leave an offering of food or drink in front of a shrine for no more than three days. It's best not to leave the offerings out long enough for them to become moldy, and if they do start to go bad, throw them away or somewhere in nature to decompose (minus any plastic of course!) Sometimes you might feel compelled to eat part of an offering, especially if Loki wants to share or feels you need some of the energy of the offering (which becomes holy once it belongs to a god). But aside from that, there are no take-backs!

Offerings for Loki might include hard alcohol, tealight candles, meats of any kind, spicy foods and peppers, candy, or toys. Many Lokeans experience a side of Loki that is whimsical and even childlike, though that certainly doesn't mean he isn't a god that can be serious or shouldn't be taken seriously. Use your intuition with giving offerings, and always use respect. Loki can be playful, but don't forget that he's a god.

Chapter 5

Lundr Lævíss: The Tree of Deceits

Óðinn, Hænir, and Loki were traveling together in the wilderness. They were starting to get hungry when they came across a herd of oxen. Killing one of them, they put it into an earth oven to cook. When they thought that it was done, they opened the oven and found the meat was still raw. They put it back in, and a second time opened the oven to find it as raw as before. They were discussing what they thought could be wrong with the meat, when above them they heard a voice who said that he was the one responsible for the meat not being able to cook. The three gods looked up into the branches of a tall oak tree, and saw that it was a massive eagle. The eagle offered to cook the meat for them, if they would give him his fill of the ox. The gods agreed, so the eagle flew down from the tree, sat on the oven, and quickly began to devour the meat. Loki became angry that there would be none left for him, and he took a wooden pole and drove it at the eagle's body as hard as he could. The eagle flew up into the air with the pole stuck to him, and Loki (like the flame at the end of a torch) was stuck to the pole and unable to let go. The eagle dragged Loki against the ground, into trees, against rocks, until he pled for mercy. The eagle, who was really the giant Þjazi in an eagle's shape, told him he would only let him go if Loki agreed to bring him the goddess Iðunn and her apples of immortality. Loki agreed, and Þjazi finally dropped him so he could return to his traveling companions.

At the agreed time, Loki lured Iðunn away from Ásgarðr and into the forest, telling her that he had found some interesting apples there. He asked her to bring her own apples with her so that they could compare them, which she did. As they were walking, Þjazi appeared in his eagle shape and carried Iðunn and her apples away to his home in Jötunheimr, the realm of the giants. With Iðunn and her apples of immortality gone, the gods began to grow grey and weak with age. They held an emergency meeting, and found that the last time Iðunn had been seen was when she was leaving Ásgarðr with Loki. The gods dragged Loki into the council, and threatened him with death or injury (as usual) if he didn't get Iðunn back for them. Loki agreed, and borrowed Freyja's falcon cloak to fly to Þjazi's home. When Loki got there, Þjazi was away, but Iðunn was there alone. Loki transformed her into a nut, and carried her in his claws back to Ásgarðr. When Þjazi returned and realized Iðunn was gone, he flew after Loki in his eagle shape as fast as he could. Meanwhile, the gods had prepared loads of wood shavings along the walls of Ásgarðr. When Þjazi tried to follow Loki over the wall, the gods lit the wood shavings and burned Þjazi's feathers, killing him when he fell to the ground.

The story of Iðunn's abduction is an old one that seems to hold many layers of symbolism. The version of it that we know comes from a poem called *Haustlöng* ("autumn-long"), which is attributed to the Norwegian skald Þjóðólfr of Hvinir, possibly written around 900 AD, and preserved in Snorri Sturluson's *Skaldskaparmal*[16]. The story seems to begin with what resembles an animal sacrifice and burnt offering. We know that cows were among the animals that were offered to the gods in ancient times, as remnants of their bones have been found with other animals such as pigs, horses, and sheep in ritual sites such as the Borg farm in Östergötland, Sweden. In Snorri's *Saga Hákonar góða*, we are given a description of what a heathen blót (which traditionally meant an animal sacrifice) may have looked like. Snorri described blót as a ritual where animals were ritually killed, their blood was sprinkled over the temple walls and altar to feed and strengthen the gods, and the meat was boiled in kettles and shared with the assembled community.

Loki, Óðinn, and Hænir seem to be in the process of one of these god-feasts when they are interrupted by a chaotic force in the shape of the Jötunn Þjazi. He carries Loki away from the blót, perhaps symbolic of the ritual fire used to cook the sacrifice (as he is trapped at the end of a stick much like the flame at the end of a torch), and makes him promise to bring him the only thing that keeps the gods immortal: The goddess Iðunn's apples. While it's tempting to take the author of *Haustlöng* at face value, his use of the word "apples" to describe what is keeping the gods immortal, it may be there is some subtle word-play at work here. In Snorri's list of kennings in *Skaldskaparmál*, he tells us that the heart can be poetically referred to as *"corn or stone or apple or nut or ball or the like"*[17].

It would then appear highly intentional on Snorri's part that the goddess Iðunn's apples would be carried away from the gods by Þjazi, then she herself would be carried back to the gods in the form of a nut: both apple and nut being kennings for the heart. A possible interpretation for this story is one in which Loki, who is often the gift-bringer of the gods, is symbolic of either a ritual fire or a ceremonial function that carries life-giving sacrifices to the gods. This is why he is the god that Þjazi abducts when he wants these offerings for himself: Loki is the only vehicle through which he can receive them. Hearts in particular seemed to have possessed some kind of supernatural or spiritual significance in the Old Norse mind, as in *Eiríks saga rauða* (The Saga of Erik the Red) the seeress Þorbjörg requires a porridge made of goat's milk and the hearts of all of the animals that lived in the settlement before she is able to go into a trance, speak to the spirits, and gain knowledge of the future. Perhaps hearts were seen as the special food of the gods and that is why she needed to eat them to gain access to their world. Loki's connection to hearts and fire appears in another highly fragmented story contained in the Eddic Poem *Hyndluljóð* ("The Song of Hyndla"), where he eats the burnt heart of an unnamed woman and gives birth to a brood of troll women or witches.

While this story places Loki yet again in the role of a trickster, deceiver, and problem solver, it also seems to place him in connection to a role as a messenger and deliverer of the god's sacrifices. The theme of sacrifice is one which occurs a great deal in Loki's mythos, and it seems to be Loki's nature to take something valuable, destroy or otherwise remove it, and then replace it with something better (or at least different). This circular nature of destroying something in the physical world in order to send it into the spirit world and thereby gain something new from the spirit world is at the very heart of the magic of sacrifice.

Making Lokean Prayer Beads

While physical hearts may have played a role in Old Norse magic and ritual, 21st century devotees of Loki also view his connection to hearts as metaphorical. Loki may be viewed as a god who helps us get to the heart of who we truly are. He is also perceived as a good who has the ability to awaken the flames of devotion in our hearts: love perhaps being the most important gateway through which the gods can be approached.

In this section, you will be creating a set of prayer beads to help structure a devotional practice. Prayer beads are a spiritual tool that are used in many different world religions: Catholicism, Buddhism, Hinduism, Islam, and others. They are a meditation tool that you can use to help remember specific prayers, say a certain number of prayers, or otherwise put your mind in a devotional, meditative state. By focusing your mind on a prayer or mantra, you are on one hand helping to silence your mental chatter to focus it fully on your devotions, and on another hand speaking words of power and intensifying that power through repetition. When the mind isn't fretting or doubting, it allows room for love to pour forth from the heart. This can create a mild, ecstatic state which is a bridge through which the divine can be communed with on a one-on-one basis.

The number of beads and types of beads you choose to use

can be totally personal. You might refer to the previous chapter and choose beads made of a stone significant to Loki. Otherwise, wood beads, glass beads, bones, seeds, or anything else can be used. All that matters is that the beads are strung in such a way as to be counted easily; usually in a circle.

A Simple Loki Devotional

Before beginning this practice, it's best to establish an altar of some kind that you can comfortably sit in front of. If that just means using a nightstand that's been cleaned and sitting on the edge of a bed, that will work. Functionality is more important than extravagance in this case.

Use your cleansing ritual to purify the space you'll be performing your devotional in, arranging your lit Loki candle, your recels, and your Snaptun Stone image on your altar space when you've finished. It would be a good idea to offer Loki a drink or some food before beginning, saying a prayer for him to be present with you during your practice.

When you've got everything settled, hold your beads in your dominant hand, holding the individual beads with your middle and ring finger, and using your thumb to count them one at a time. With each bead, you can either chant one of Loki's *heiti* (poetic names), a prayer of your own creation, or you can use this simple mantra I've taken from the Eddic Poem *Lokasenna*:

Heill ver þú nú, Loki (Hail ver thoo noo, Loki)
Hail to you now, Loki

I find it's best to extend this phrase into a song or chant as you say it, which helps to induce a more meditative state. As you chant, keep your focus on the flame, the incense, and your image of Loki. Feel your heart opening and becoming a door through which the god can enter. Don't overthink this or try to force something to happen. Just allow yourself to feel love and devotion. When you've finished your chanting, sit in silence for a few moments and observe how you're feeling. Allow your mind to be still and see if Loki has anything he wants to say to you or any thoughts he wants to inspire you with.

Chapter 6

Lokabrenna: Loki's Torch

Not long after the gods had regained Iðunn, Þjazi's fearsome daughter Skaði appeared in Ásgarðr dressed in a helmet, chainmail, and armed with weapons of war. Though she wanted vengeance for her father's death, the gods offered her compensation in exchange for peace. They offered her a husband, who she was only allowed to choose by looking at his feet and nothing else. The gods lined up and she chose the most beautiful feet, hoping they belonged to Baldr, but instead she had chosen Njorðr, who rules over the motion of the wind and the sea.

She also asked for something she didn't think the gods would be able to offer her after her father's death: laughter. Rising to the challenge, Loki tied a cord around the beard of a nanny-goat and the other end around his testicles. They drew each other back and forth in a ridiculous tug-of-war and each one cried out when the other one pulled. Finally Loki fell into Skaði's lap in such a ridiculous fashion that she laughed despite herself. Thus her compensation was complete and she was ever after counted among the goddesses of Ásgarðr.

The strange, lewd episode of Skaði's payment is one which reveals one of Loki's most endearing qualities: his ability to create laughter. Comedy is one of the gifts of the many trickster figures throughout history, and it often has held an important social function in many different cultures. Through the leans of comedy, we are able to defuse emotionally charged issues enough to really look at them. Sometimes it is used to challenge unnecessary boundaries, and sometimes it's used to point out boundaries that shouldn't be crossed. Humor has also often been used as a weapon to call out political injustice and hypocrisy.

The Medieval court jester was the only figure who was allowed to criticize the royal family without punishment, using their humor as a mirror for serious political and social issues. Loki's humor and irreverence are qualities that have earned him much love from his devotees, and like other trickster figures his foibles often carry deeper lessons and meanings. While Loki is counted among the gods, he hardly seems to be beholden to them (or to be all that impressed with them in most cases), and it is usually only through threats of violence that he can finally be persuaded to obey them. The people who wrote down the Eddic myths and poems use Loki more than once to reveal the god's follies and weaknesses, pointing out the futility of trying to control destiny and nature. Loki could be said to represent the chaotic element in any natural system which lends it unpredictability. But while Loki is a god who will teach you to question outside authority, he is also a god who will teach you to see the humor in yourself. He may also be there to turn the joke on you when you're taking yourself far too seriously, are acting in arrogance, or trying to direct forces that are outside of your ability to control.

While Loki's penchant for humor is being displayed in this story, it is also likely that there's an element of symbolism in this strange interaction between he and Skaði, who is a skier and a huntress associated with the forces of winter. Some scholars have suggested that some rite of castration within Skaði's cultus is being suggested here[18]. Because the star Sirius was known as *Lokabrenna* in Iceland[19], I have also considered that this story may bear some connection to a brief description of a ritual from Hedeby (a Danish trading post in the Viking Age)), recorded by the Spanish traveller Al Tartushi in the 10th century. Al Tartushi claimed that the inhabitants of Hedeby worshiped the star Sirius, impaling sacrificed animals on poles at the door to their houses (including cattle, rams, goats, or pigs) so that their neighbors would be aware that they were making a sacrifice in honor of their deity. Who that deity was remains unspoken[20].

Perhaps the story of Loki tying a goat to his "pole" harkens back to some older sacrificial ritual that has since been forgotten. Sirius was known as the "dog star" by the Greeks and Romans due to its prominent placement in the constellation Canis Major. Its visibility in the eastern horizon at dawn during July and August was seen as the cause of the increased, uncomfortable heat in the Mediterranean world. These months came to be known as the "dog days of summer". The name Sirius comes from the Greek word *seírios,* meaning "scorching". If the ancient Scandinavians held any such association with Sirius, this could be seen as relevant to an interpretation of Loki "warming" Skaði (perhaps representative of the winter) with laughter. In either case, the Danish worship of Sirius seems significant to Loki, especially if the star was also known as *Lokabrenna* in that region (but sadly, we will probably never know for sure).

A Lokabrenna Ritual

The following ritual is intended to introduce Sirius as a source of power and inspiration for Loki devotees. Lokabrenna is a bright star, which can be located by using Orion's Belt as an arrow that points downward and to the left. The first brightest star you see in that direction is Loki's torch (actually, it's the brightest star in the night sky).

On a night where the sky is clear and the star is visible, go outside (with your Snaptun Stone if you choose). Place your Loki image somewhere safe where it can be touched by the star's light. When you've found Sirius, take a moment to breathe and gather your focus on it, perhaps using the Loki chant you learned in the previous chapter as you do. Still standing, raise your arms up towards the star, and as you have done with your fire breathing, imagine that you are breathing in white star-fire from Lokabrenna. Feel this light filling your body, burning away any illness, emotional distress, or impurities within you that you want to release. As you breath in more and more of this light,

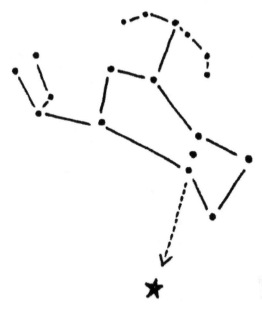

imagine it beginning to envelop your body in a protective sphere of white fire, driving away any harmful influences from your person. When you've gathered enough energy from Lokabrenna, sit in silence for a few moments and allow it to settle. Observe any thoughts or feelings that might arise. When your practice is complete, close with something to the effect of:

May your torch always be my light in the darkness. Hail Loki

If you feel jittery or want to feel more grounded, hold your Snaptun Stone image and allow any excess energy you want to release to flow into the image through your breath. "Feeding" your stone in this way, either through energy or offerings will help to strengthen it as a spiritual anchor for Loki.

Chapter 7

Goða Dolgr: The Enemy of the Gods

Aside from his wife Sigyn in Asgarðr, Loki had a lover in Jötunheimr named Angrboða, the "distress bringer". With her he had three children: Fenrir the monstrous wolf, Jörmungandr the world serpent, and Hel the goddess of death, half of whose body is beautiful while the other is a rotting corpse. When the Æsir discovered that these three children were being raised in Jötunheimr, they traced prophecies to them that said they would be the cause of great disaster. Óðinn sent the gods to collect the children and bring them to him. Jörmungandr he threw into the sea, where the serpent grew so enormous that he encircled the world until he could bite his own tail. Hel was thrown into Niflheimr, where she was left to care for the spirits of the dead who had died of sickness or old age. The Æsir brought the wolf home with them, until Fenrir grew so enormous that they chose to deceive him into being bound with a magical fetter forged by the dwarves. The wolf lays bound and waiting on an island named Lyngvi, just as his siblings lay in wait until they will escape their imprisonment at Ragnarök and will go to battle against the gods.

Loki's role as father (and mother) of monsters is one of his most complex aspects, and just as Loki brought the gods their most valuable weapons after cutting off Sif's hair, he is also paradoxically the father of their most dangerous foes. In his book *Trickster Makes This World*, Lewis Hyde examines how in Native American folklore in particular, trickster is often the creator of our world. However, this isn't an idealistic world, but the world as it truly is: beautiful, but often chaotic, senseless, and ultimately devouring. The enormous appetites of trickster influenced the world he created, where in order for life to continue other life must be eaten. Trickster is also often the bringer of either gifts or unintentional calamity to the world. In Hesiod's *Theogony*, Prometheus tricks Zeus into instituting the practice of sacrifice, where humans eat the meat of sacrificial animals and dedicate the inedible parts to the gods. Zeus tries to withhold fire from man so they are unable to cook the sacrificial meat (not dissimilar from the way in which Þjazi prevents Loki and his companions from cooking their food), but Prometheus steals the fire back and gives it to humankind. In retribution for this act, Zeus creates the first woman, whose descendants are said to bring torment into the world[21].

Much like his Greek cousin Prometheus, Loki also indirectly produces a progeny of sinister female beings. There are 15 stanzas at the end of the Eddic poem *Hyndluljóð* that are referred to as *Völuspá in skamma* (The Short Seeress's Prophecy), which is a smaller, condensed vision of the end of the world. In Stanza 41, we are told that Loki ate the burnt heart of an unnamed woman, and thereby became pregnant and gave birth to all of the world's *flagð*, which can be translated as "ogresses", "giantesses", "female monsters", or "witches". While the owner of the heart which impregnated Loki remains unknown, the nature of the children he gives birth to may reflect the nature of the heart's owner, as other Scandinavian folktales exist where a woman eats a heart and becomes pregnant with a child similar to the hearts' owner[22]. Regardless of the original context, those interested in Traditional Witchcraft may find it of interest that Loki is counted among deities who are regarded as a "witch father" (or in this case, "witch mother").

Loki's three most famous children are arguably Fenrir, Jörmungandr, and Hel: all three of which play prominent roles in the destruction of the world at Ragnarök. As Loki is a deity that is often connected to themes of fire and sacrifice, his devouring nature may be reflected in these three children, who themselves seem to embody the predatory essence of the natural world and the all-consuming nature of death itself. Fenrir embodies the devouring nature of the animal kingdom, Jörmungandr embodies the devouring nature of the sea, and Hel is the grave that devours all things.These three beings seem to be agents of time and destiny, through which all things eventually meet their end. Their chthonic natures also point to darker aspects of Loki's character, who as a bound god of sacrifice holds many ties to the underworld himself.

In modern times, many worshippers of Loki who have been made to feel monstrous or "othered" in their own communities have identified with Loki's role as the parent of the unconventional and misunderstood. Loki doesn't reject his more terrifying children, and in fact, seems to deeply understand the important role that they play in the function of the world. In any organic system, life and creation cannot go unchecked without death and decay. Due to Loki's resistance to maintaining any kind of recognizable gender roles, he has also been adopted as a patron deity by many people in the LGBTQ community, who themselves have often been the victims of oppression, misunderstanding, and fear-mongering.

Metaphorically, Loki can be viewed as a deity who brings our shadows or the shadows of our culture out into the light. While the gods try to banish and suppress these "demons", it is only prolonging their inevitable escape, which ultimately leads to the destruction and resurrection of the world.

A Demon Work Ritual

A "demon" in the context of this ritual isn't an invading spirit that needs to be cast out of us. A demon is an internal construct that is created when we attempt to shame, cast aside, or otherwise suppress aspects of ourselves. A demon might be a suppressed desire, a shameful memory, an attribute that we were taught was undesirable, or any number of things we have chosen to reject about ourselves. Much like the gods in this story, we cast them down into dark places in our subconscious, hoping that if they're out of sight they won't be able to influence our lives. However, this suppression often only leads to an explosion later, when these demons find way to lash out in our lives and create havoc for us and those around us. Rejecting and cutting off parts of ourselves isn't a functional solution for long.

This is a simple ritual intended to introduce you to one of these demons, the goal being that by understanding what this demon is, where it came from, and how it effects your life you can circumvent self-destructive behaviors or attitudes that you've been enacting unconsciously. Bear in mind, ritual work is in no way a replacement for therapy. If you choose to try this exercise and it brings up heavy things, don't be afraid to seek professional assistance to help you process them.

What you will need:
Your Loki candle (and extra candles if you desire)
Lokean recels
A mirror
1 unlit tealight candle
A notebook and pen to write with

Use your cleansing ritual to purify the space in which you'll be working. In the ritual space, you will need to arrange a mirror and a place to sit in front of it. This can be a full-length mirror or a hand-held mirror; it doesn't matter what kind as long as you can sit comfortably in front of it for as long as you need to. You'll want to turn the lights in the room off, and ideally this is a ritual you'll practice at night. The only light in the room should be coming from your Loki candle, adding other candles as well if you want more light (please stay safe/aware when meditating around flames!) The candles can either be arranged in front of the mirror, around you, or somewhere behind you. Keep the notebook and pen near you in case you need to jot down insights you want to remember.

Settle yourself in front of your mirror, and start a rhythmic breathing pattern to calm your mind. I like to count to four on my inhale, hold it for four, exhale for four, and then hold for four again. When you feel you've reached a calm, meditative state, look yourself in the eyes in the mirror and say a prayer out-loud to the effect of:

Hail Loki, father of monsters and bringer of light. I ask you to send me one of your three children, be it Hel, the serpent or the wolf, to guide me to a part of myself that I've rejected. In your name, let them lead me to this demon and show me where it came from, so that I can begin the journey of healing and self-knowledge.

For the sake of this exercise, each of Loki's children by Angrboða will help lead you to a specific type of demon. Fenris will lead you to your demons born from anger, Jörmungandr will lead you to your demons created by grief, and Hel will lead you to your demons created by fear. Though these three gods can be terrifying, they are also sources of powerful insight. Hel in particular as the caretaker of the dead has a motherly, compassionate side. She is a devouring goddess, but the living half of her face is also a promise of rebirth.

As you gaze at yourself in the mirror, allow your eyes to unfocus, and in your mind's eye, see one of Loki's children come to you in the mirror. Whichever one appears will give a hint as to which of your demons you will be confronting. Listen to their words, and allow them to guide you into the mirror and towards the secret part of yourself where the demon waits. Ask them to reveal to you where and why the demon was born, how that demon causes you to act, and what it does to your life. Bear in mind, this demon is not an exterior enemy that you need to destroy. It is a part of yourself, and the only way a demon such as this can be tamed is to acknowledge it. Through accepting yourself in all your parts, this demon can be transformed into an ally towards self-knowledge. Not all demons have good ideas, and acceptance doesn't mean handing the reigns of your life over to it. But with this new self-awareness, you will be able to act with clear intention in your life and not from an unconscious place of wounding.

See if Loki's child has any advice for you on how to manage and integrate the lessons of this demon, then ask them to lead you back up from the darkness and back to your waking consciousness. Thank them for the gift of knowledge they've given you. Before you leave your place in front of the mirror, take a few minutes to look at yourself in the eyes. Tell yourself out-loud anything you needed to hear but didn't when your demon was born.

Once you have gained the knowledge you need, take the unlit tealight and hold it in both hands. Imagine that the demon is swirling inside your body like black smoke. With each exhale, imagine that the black smoke is passing out of your body, through your hands, and into the tealight. When you feel that you've completed this visualization, light the candle, saying something to the effect of:

I acknowledge my demon of _____. *With the fire of this candle, may it be illuminated and transformed.*

After this underworld descent, you might feel the desire for extra purification. If that's the case, cleansing yourself with your Loki candle and recels is a quick and easy solution.

Chapter 8

Inn Bundi Áss: The Bound God

The gods were gathered together in the hall of Ægir, the god of the sea and were having a great feast together. Only Þórr wasn't present, because he was off in the East fighting giants. Everyone was praising the excellence of Ægir's servants Eldir and Fimafeng. Loki couldn't bear to hear their praise, and killed Fimafeng in front of the assembly. There was a great outcry, and the gods drove Loki out of the hall and into the woods, then returned to their drinking. Soon, Loki returned and met Eldir outside the hall, and convinced him to let him back inside. The gods gave Loki a chilly reception until he invoked Óðinn's oath to him that he would not drink unless Loki was offered a drink as well. Loki was given his drink, and then began to call out all of the gods in turn: reminding them of every shameful deed they had ever performed. It wasn't until Þórr appeared that he could be silenced, and as he was driven away from Ægir's hall he cursed it so that it would be consumed in flames.

After this incident, Loki hid himself in the waterfall of Franangr, transforming himself into the shape of a salmon. The Æsir captured him there (some say with the same fish-net that Loki himself invented). Loki's two children with his wife Sigyn weren't spared their father's punishment: Váli was transformed into a wolf who tore his brother Narvi apart. Loki was carried to a cave, where he was bound to three stones with the guts of his dead son. In retribution for the death of her father, Skaði hung a poisonous snake over Loki, which dripped poison into his face. Sigyn, Loki's wife, sat with him and held a hand-basin under the stream of the poison to spare him the pain. Whenever the basin became full, she carried the poison out, leaving Loki exposed to the snake's venom. When the poison hit Loki's face he writhed so violently against his bindings that the earth would shake. This is why we have earthquakes.

The binding of Loki is one of his most famous stories, and the image of Loki bound beneath the earth with a snake dripping venom into his face is one of his most famous depictions. It even has archeological significance, as the 11th century Gosforth Cross (located in Cumbria, England) possibly contains a depiction of a bound Loki with Sigyn holding a bowl and a knotted snake to their left. This cross holds many images that resemble events at Ragnarök as described in *Völuspá* and *Gylfaginning*. This might signify an association in the artists mind between the demise of the old gods and the rise of Christianity.

The first version of Loki's binding comes from the Eddic poem *Lokasenna* which has been dated to the 10th or as late as the 12th century[23]. The second one comes to us from Snorri, either as an alternate version or one of his own invention (which will be discussed in the next chapter). *Lokasenna* means "Loki's senna", and the original purpose and tone of the poem is still uncertain. It may have been meant to be an amusing satire, as Loki engages the gods in a battle of insults. Some have also suggested that the poem was written by a Christian author as a way to disgrace the old gods through Loki's mouth[24]. Due to the format of the poem, it's also possible that it was intended to be performed as a play, as it is structured with lines and seems to contain action prompts as well. Whatever the context of the poem, the word *senna* is an interesting one. *Senna* is derived from the Old Norse word *sannr*, which means "truth"[25]. That would imply that rather than Loki getting into trouble for telling lies about the gods, his greatest punishment came as a result of telling the gods things about themselves they didn't want to hear. Loki is like the child who tells the Emperor that he has no clothes on, and many modern worshippers of Loki consider him to be a teller of unwelcome truths: especially when it's the truth that nobody wants to confront but needs to be said. Whistleblowers are often met with hostility, which was certainly true in Loki's case.

Loki's antics eventually lead him to a gruesome punishment, and his wife Sigyn is the only one who shows him any mercy. Sigyn is an enigmatic goddess, who only appears in this one surviving story. Her name has been translated to mean "victorious girlfriend"[26], which is an unusual name for a deity in such a debilitated position. Due to the strange nature of Loki's punishment, I have often thought that many of these elements are symbolic in nature, and have noticed a similarity between Loki and Sigyn's relationship and that of the Vedic gods Agni and Svāhā. Where Agni is the literal personification of ritual fire (as I suspect Loki himself may have been), his wife Svāhā is the goddess of oblation, who pours ghee and rice into her husband's flames. Through the vehicle of Agni, the gods receive their offerings and strength, just as Loki is also the gift-bringer and messenger of the gods. In this context, the image of a woman holding a bowl over her husband, a fire deity, takes on a very different tone.

In the description of *blót* in *Saga Háknonar góða*, Snorri tells us that all kinds of animals were killed, and their blood was collected in bowls. This blood was then sprinkled over the altars and walls of the temple and on the assembled worshippers. Fires were lit in the middle of the temple floor, and large kettles would be hung over them where the flesh of the animals would be boiled. A bowl would then be filled with soup, toasts to the gods were made, and soup would be eaten by the community[27]. Adding to the complexity of the symbolism in Loki's binding, according to the Eddic poem *Völuspá,* Loki is bound with Sigyn under the *hveralundi* ("kettle-grove). This may be a kenning for a hot spring, which would tie Loki to the volcanic activity under the earth: perhaps emphasizing his attributes as a chthonic deity of fire who creates earthquakes with his struggling. A second interpretation may be that the "kettle grove" in question is actually the kettles in which the animal sacrifices would be boiled during blót. This of course would mean that Loki is being equated with the fire underneath the kettles and the basin that Sigyn holds over him is symbolic of the sacrifice bowls. One could also imagine Loki's binding by the guts of his son to three stones (perhaps "stones" here is yet again being used as a kenning for "hearts") to be symbolic of the inedible organs of animal sacrifices being burned in the sacred fire during such rituals: binding the sacrificial fire to the ritual space. These bindings also bring the ropes used to delineate the vé-bönd to mind. As the story of Loki's binding evolved for Christian audiences, perhaps the liquid in Sigyn's bowl was transformed from a drink of power to one of deadly poison (i.e. something you shouldn't drink if you want to go to heaven), though of course that is only my speculation.

Many of the themes of Loki's binding also appear in Hesiod's story of Prometheus (a titan, not dissimilar from a Jötunn) who is punished for stealing mankind the fire to use in their animal sacrifices. Interestingly, Prometheus's punishment also involves binding and the ripping out of organs, as Zeus sends an eagle to where he is bound to eat his liver (which regenerates over and over) every day. The similarity between Loki and Prometheus's myths may point to a common, Indo-European motif of a fire giant being bound beneath the earth in connection to ideas of sacrifice.

Whether you choose to interpret the story of Loki's binding at face value or to read other symbolism into it, there is much to be gleaned about Loki from this story. It reveals Loki's role as the teller of inconvenient truths. For many devotees of Loki, he acts as a force in our lives that inspires self-reflection and authenticity. While he may be deceptive at times, Loki rarely tolerates it when we lie to ourselves.

Making a Blót Bowl

Sigyn is a goddess who is held in great esteem by Lokeans for her strength, strong will, and loyalty. In many ways, she might be regarded as Loki's ultimate devotee, whether you interpret her actions as a selfless act of mercy or as an act of ritual worship. As you have already read, offering bowls seem to have been of special importance to the religious rituals of the ancient Scandinavians, and I personally connect them to Sigyn. It's interesting to note that when describing Sigyn's bowl, both the author of *Lokasenna* and Snorri choose to use the word *mundlaug*, which in Old Norse translates to a hand-basin (a basin for washing your hands in). The most famous instance of a hand-basin such as this appearing in a cultural context is in the Arab traveller Ibn Fadlan's account of his encounter with who he called the Rus: a North Germanic tribe. According to Fadlan, the Rus would be offered a basin filled with water by a slave girl every day to wash their faces in[28].

Whether some kind of hidden meaning is implied in the word *mundlaug* or not, your bowl can be used for both giving offerings to Loki and for blessing water or other substances towards your own spiritual purification. You can also fill this bowl with water and use it for scrying if that is one of your talents and you need answers from the gods.

What you will need:
Your Loki candle
Lokean recels
1 wooden bowl
A dremel or wood-burner
1 lancet (or blood substitute)

Perform your cleansing ceremony in the place where you intend to work. When you've finished, take your wooden bowl and cleanse it over your Loki candle and in the smoke of the recels. This purification makes it ready to become a holy tool. Next, you will be either carving or burning this *mundlaug* stave[29] into the center of the bowl's basin:

As you create the stave, pray to Loki and Sigyn to empower your ritual bowl that it can be used as a tool to transmit offerings to the gods, to bless and purify yourself, and to seek knowledge when needed. When you've finished carving, use your lancet to get a drop of blood from your finger, dabbing it onto the stave to awaken it (wash it before its first use).

When you want to use the bowl to give liquid offerings to Loki, place your bowl on your altar in front of your lit Loki candle and Snaptun Stone image. As you pour your offering, you can say something to the effect of:

> *Sig, sig, sig*
> *Sigyn grants sure victory*
> *To worthy gods and men*
> *Through your hands pour all oblations*
> *Bring our blessed offerings*
> *To the bright burden of your arms*
> *Gateway through which the gods*
> *Gladly feast and grow in strength*
> *Gift for gift, may be ever gain*
> *The grace of our elder Kin.*
> *Hail Loki, Hail Sigyn.*

If you wish to use the bowl as a tool of personal cleansing, light your Loki candle and fill the bowl with water. Perform your fire breathing, and with each exhale imagine that you are gathering and breathing Loki's flames into the water, charging it until it is glowing with bright, golden light. To finish blessing the water, hold your hands above it, and use this washing charm[30] that I adopted from the *Galdrabók* (an Icelandic grimoire dated to around the 16th century) and altered for this purpose:

> *I wash myself in the dew and dales in Loki's bright brilliance. I wash myself from the ill-will of any enemies or magic spells. I wash myself from all obstacles, missteps, and wrath. May the world bless me with good friends and benefactors. May the land bless me with good food and provisions. May everything be good for me that I need to do, say, or think. This I ask from you, Loki and Sigyn, so that*

everyone who sees me on this day may turn to me with loving eyes. May all misfortune, bad luck, wickedness and wiles be turned away from me. May all those who want to betray me in words, deeds, or sorcery vanish and be turned away from me. Hear my prayer my lord and lady. I believe in, and trust you for all good things. Loki, spider, please keep the threads of my fate untangled. Hail.

After you have blessed the water, you can either sprinkle it on yourself, drink it, or add it to a shower or ritual bath.

Chapter 9

Hveðrung: The Roarer

According to Snorri, Loki's binding took place for a very different reason. It was said that Óðinn's son Baldr was having dreams about his own death. He was so beloved by all of the gods that his mother Frigg went to all of the beings in creation and made them swear oaths that they would never harm him. When this was done and confirmed, the gods took turns throwing objects at Baldr, who was now immune to any damage. This turned into a source of entertainment for Baldr and the Æsir. Only Loki, who hates stagnation, was unhappy to see that Baldr could no longer be harmed. Loki transformed himself into a woman and went to Frigg's hall. He feigned ignorance at the activities of the gods, and Frigg explained how she had made everything promise not to harm her son. When the woman pressed her to know if she had really received an oath from everything, Frigg admitted that she hadn't asked for an oath from the mistletoe, as it seemed too young and small for her to demand an oath from it. When Frigg said that, the woman disappeared, and Loki took off for the woods to gather mistletoe to bring to the assembly.

When Loki reached the assembly where the gods were throwing things at Baldr, he noticed that Baldr's blind brother Höðr wasn't throwing anything, and he offered to help guide his hand to join in the fun. With Loki's help, Höðr fired the mistletoe at Baldr, and when it shot through him he fell to the ground dead. The gods tried to strike a deal with the goddess Hel to release Baldr back to Ásgarðr, she agreed on the condition that all things in the world shed tears for him. Only one being in all the worlds didn't cry for Baldr: the giantess Þökk ("thanks"), who was actually Loki in disguise. It was for this reason that Snorri tells us Loki was captured and bound.

It is said that in the end of days, Midgaðr would be cast into a "wolf-age", where brother would fight brother, the world would be enveloped in an endless winter, and all morality would be abandoned. It is in this age that Loki and his children break their bonds, arriving in Ásgarðr leading an army of the dead, monsters, and a legion of fire giants from Muspelheimr. In their wake the world tree itself would burn and most gods and humans would be killed in the final battle at Ragnarök. But in the wake of this destruction a new, better world would arise, and Baldr, who had been preserved in the world of the dead, would return to be its ruler.

While Loki has his aspects as a comical prankster, it would be a mistake to think that Loki is harmless. Loki's powerful role as world-breaker is an important and deeply symbolic aspect to his nature that shouldn't be ignored. One of Loki's bynames is Hveðrungr, which has been translated to mean "roarer". This name might evoke images of Loki in his role as destroyer, burning all of creation to the ground in roaring flames. Along with being the spark of life in the blood, the forge-fire of creativity, and the sacred fire of sacrifice, he is the raging forest fire and the roaring volcano, devouring everything in its path. He is the closer of worlds that lights the funeral pyre of a dying Midgarðr ravaged by wars and endless winters so that a new world may be reborn in its place.

Of all the deities in Norse mythology, Loki seems to have the closest relationship to the fire giants of Muspelheimr (sometimes called the Sons of Muspel), and it's possible he should be counted among them. According to Snorri, Surtr is the giant who guards the boundary of Muspelheimr with a fiery sword, which he will use to burn the worlds down at the end of time. In the Eddic Poem *Fjölvinnsmál*, Loki is said to forge a sword the author calls Lævateinn ("destruction wand") in Niflhel, the realm of his daughter. Surtr's wife Sinmara keeps in an iron box with nine locks: presumably until he will use it at Ragnarök.

Loki's role in Ragnarök and Baldr's death are the primary

reasons he tends to be so maligned within the Heathen community in particular. With all of that being said, it is important to point out that Snorri's version of Baldr's death at Loki's hand isn't necessarily the oldest or most authentic. Saxo Grammaticus was a Danish theologian and historian, who wrote his 16-volume *Gesta Danorum* ("Deeds of the Danes") around the end of the 12th century, very close to the same time Snorri was finishing his Edda. Saxo told a version of Baldr's death where Baldr and Höðr (in his version, not blind, a god, or Baldr's brother) were mortal enemies, fighting for the hand of a woman named Nanna (who Snorri describes as Baldr's wife). Höðr eventually kills Baldr with a sword called Mistleteinn, though in this version Loki is nowhere to be seen. This may mean that there were different regional versions of this same story, even in pre-Christian times.

Regardless, Snorri's version remains the most well-known and retold, and contains its own Lokean wisdom. It has been observed by some modern Heathens that because Baldr was killed he will be preserved in Hel's hall and avoid the carnage occurring during Ragnarök. Because of this, he is able to step into his role as the new leader of the gods when the dust has cleared and the world has been reborn. The theme of death and resurrection as a metaphor for personal enlightenment and mastery is theme that arises more than once in Norse cosmology. Óðinn describes in the Eddic poem *Hávamál* how he hung and died on the world-tree Yggdrasil before gaining knowledge of the runes. One can see how Loki's actions created an underworld initiation for Baldr, in which he has to die and re-ascend from the world of the dead to claim rulership over the new world.

The Druids viewed mistletoe as a healing herb, which hasn't been lost on many people examining Loki's weapon of choice. It's also notable that in Snorri's account of Baldr's funeral, Óðinn places the magical, replicating ring Draupnir (a possible symbol of eternal life) on Baldr's funeral pyre when Loki was the one who acquired it for him in the first place. It's almost as if he and

Loki had Baldr's resurrection after Ragnarök planned all along. In the myth of Baldr, Loki can be understood as an initiator: one who takes Baldr out of his place of safety, which has become a bubble of weakness, and stagnation, and destroys his old self so that a greater self might arise. This has largely been a thankless act for Loki, but perhaps he's willing to be the fall-guy towards the goal of the world's transformation and evolution.

A Sovereignty Blessing

Claiming a sense of personal sovereignty has been at the heart of my walk with Loki through the years I've worshipped and studied him. For me, that means learning to own myself for who I really am (the good and the bad), so that I can be my own guiding force in my life and make choices that help me walk in personal integrity. There are times in our lives where we are all a little like Baldr: we want to remain sheltered and protected, and might look to other people or institutes (religious or otherwise) to keep us safe from chaos and the unknown. However, Loki represents the unexpected and the unpredictable, and the idea that there is a shield that can protect us from life is an illusion he can't help but destroy. Life's many upsets have a way of destroying our sense of control, and it is in those moments that we awaken to the reality that the only control we have in life is how we choose to perceive and react. Claiming that ownership rather than looking for it outside of myself was one of the more important lessons Loki had to teach me. Over and over again Loki shows us the impermanence of unpredictability of life: what matters is what we choose to do about it.

Claiming sovereignty over your life isn't as easy as it sounds, and our culture encourages us to give our power and integrity away to other things and people all the time in tiny ways. There's no fix-all ritual to help you step into your power, but I'm including ritual you can add to your spiritual practice when you need a reminder of who wears the crown in your own life.

Making Loki Oil

1/2 oz of Jojoba oil

3 pinches of powdered dragon's blood resin or 3 drops of dragon's blood oil

2 drops of black pepper essential oil

1 pinch of mullein leaf or flowers

1 pinch or red pepper flakes

1 pinch of mistletoe

1 small pinch of sulphur

A small piece of snake skin sheds (if you can acquire some)

Combine these ingredients together in a small bottle and leave it near your Snaptun Stone image overnight. Ask Loki to bless the oil so that you can use it in your work with him. While this oil can be used in self-blessings, you can also use it to anoint your sacred objects and empower items and places with Loki's energy.

What you will need:

Your Loki candle

Your Loki oil

This ritual is short and sweet, and can easily be incorporated into your devotional work or into any spiritual, daily practice. Light your Loki candle and perform your fire breathing for a few moments. Meditate on Loki's fire burning away any emotional, physical, or mental obstacles that are currently impeding your sense of sovereignty and worth. As those obstacles burn away, focus on the fire within you: the flame that is at the core your own divine self. When you are ready say something to the effect of:

In the name of Loki, may the work of my hands be blessed
(use a little bit of oil to draw a Kenaz[31] rune on each of your hands)

In the name of Loki, may the work of my mind be blessed
(draw Kenaz on your forehead)
In the name of Loki, may the work of my heart be blessed
(draw Kenaz over your heart)
In the name of Loki, I claim the crown of my own sovereignty

(rub a small amount oil into your first three fingers, then rub them from your eyebrows to the back of your head, as if you're pulling something into your head)

Sit for a moment, and imagine a crown of flames burning over your head and Kenaz glowing bright red in the places you drew it. When you're ready, walk through the rest of your day with integrity.

Chapter 10

Gammleið: The Vulture's Road

Loki, Þórr and his servant Þjalfi had finally reached the hall of the giant Utgarðr-Loki ("out-world Loki") after many trials and tribulations. When they reached the hall, Utgarðr-Loki told them that only people of exceptional skill were allowed to stay there with he and his company. Loki, who was famished from the journey, was the first to speak up. He boasted that nobody would be able to eat their food quicker than he could. Utgarðr-Loki accepted his challenge, and pulled out a trencher filled with meat. A man named Logi was called from the bench, and he sat on one end while Loki sat at the other. They both ate as quickly as they could and met in the middle. Loki had eaten all the meat off the bones, but Logi had eaten the meat, the bones, and the trencher. While Loki lost the contest, it was revealed later that Logi was actually the personification of wildfire, which eats faster than anything.

Loki's byname Gammleið is an interesting one, and it translates to vulture (*gammr*) road (*leið*). On one hand, this seems to relate to Loki's relationship with the air. His name Loptr relates to the sky, and according to Snorri he possesses shoes that allow him to walk over air and water. It may be that by calling him the road of the vulture, Loki is being equated with a force that either embodies or travels through the air. I have also considered that the specific choice of the vulture in his name may point to his function as a deity of destruction with many inferred connections to the underworld.

A hint pointing towards this aspect of Loki's nature may be hidden within the story of his eating contest with Logi. The word *logi* literally means "fire" in Old Norse, but that doesn't mean that only one type of fire existed in the minds of ancient

Scandinavians. In Vedic culture and other Indo-European cultures of which the Germanic peoples are one branch, there is often a distinction between mundane fires, the fire of the sun, and fires used for ritualistic purposes. So what kind of fire does that make Loki? If we are to imagine Loki as embodying the ritual fire who carries burnt offerings to the gods, he can also be imagined as the cremation fire who carries souls to the gods as well. In Bronze Age Scandinavia, cremation was the primary form of funerary practice. The bones weren't damaged in the cremation fire, but were removed from the pyre after burning and washed before they were placed in an urn and buried. The careful removal of the bones from the ashes may have symbolized freeing the spirit from the physical world. It wasn't until the Iron Age that the practice of removing the bones of the death from the funeral pyre fell out of fashion, and cremation itself began to be abandoned for more lavish burials[32]. Loki's inability to eat the bones in the trencher may be a hint, revealing him to be the embodiment of cremation and sacrificial fire, rather than mundane fire that can eat anything. Though we don't know for sure how the ancient Scandinavians conduced their sacrifices, the story of Loki and Logi also brings to mind the story of how Prometheus instituted the Greek tradition of the sacrificial bones being uneaten and left to the gods.

In his work *Ynglinaga saga*, Snorri tells us that it was Óðinn who instituted the practice of cremation among the Æsir[33]. There is no surviving story to tell us how or why Óðinn made Loki his blood brother, but one could imagine that a deity who instituted cremation might want to make the sacred fire itself his ally. Following this interpretation, when we are told in *Lokasenna* that Óðinn swore never to drink unless Loki was given a drink as well might be very literal: Óðinn and the other gods can't receive a sacrifice unless it passes through the sacrificial fire first, as we learned in Snorri's description of blót. In *Sörla þáttr*, a short narrative in the Icelandic manuscript *Flateyjarbók* (14th century), we are told that Loki left his parents to go live as Óðinn's right hand man, and as a god who is sustained through war, death, and sacrifice, what better ally for Óðinn than the sacred fire. The fact that Loki is equated with vultures, in particular in his name Gammleið, might reinforce his connection to death and specifically cremation. Much like the cremation fires of the Bronze Age, vultures are also devourers of flesh and refuse, leaving behind nothing but bones. From a spiritual perspective, Loki can be experienced as a deity who can burn away the limiting, the unnecessary, and the sickness in our own lives. It may be that this level of symbolism was intended by Snorri, who tells us that Baldr was cremated on his own ship after his death: Loki being Baldr's personal gateway into the underworld in more than one form. While these transformations from one state to another can be painful and misunderstood, they also have the ability to free us and progress our growth.

Utgarðr-Loki is an unusual character who Snorri offers us very little explanation for. He seems very similar to Loki Laufeyjarson in many ways: he is a jötunn who rules a large hall in Utgarðr; "out world" being a way to describe the place outside of the known, safer world of family, order, and culture. Like Loki Laufyejarson, he is a shapeshifter and a magician who can deceive the mind, and a trickster who deceives Þórr and his companions into battling with insurmountable forces in order to secretly test their strength. Snorri presents him as a being who is separate from Loki Laufeyjarson, while Saxo's Utgarthilocus is found bound in a cave surrounded by the dripping of poison and he may have considered them to be the same person. Whether Utgarðr-Loki should be considered an aspect or shadow self of Loki is debatable. It may also be that they were considered to be two different figures whose myths were eventually conflated by Snorri and other authors. Like most things where Loki is concerned, there's no clear answer.

Lokablót (A Loki Blót)

The following is a model for a blót (sacrifice) for Loki that can be performed either by yourself or with a group. Because fire sacrifice has become so central to my own understanding of who and what Loki is, this ritual will require that you have access to a place to safely burn offerings. Ideally, an outdoor fire-pit would be the best location for this type of ritual. An indoor fireplace is also an appropriate choice. In his work *Loke in the Younger Tradition*, The Danish folklorist Axel Olrik collected a variety of surviving folk customs about Loki (who by the 19th century had been diminished into a mischievous spirit). A folk custom he recorded in Telemarken, Norway, says that when people boiled milk they would throw the skin into the fire as a sacrifice to "Lokje". These folk customs suggest that feeding Loki as the fire of the hearth has at least a more recent historical precedent. However, if you absolutely have no way to use a large fire, you can pour your offerings into a vessel surrounded by candles as a symbolic gesture.

There is a spiritual and philosophical reasoning behind fire sacrifice, at the root of which is the idea that in the natural world, all things are gained through one thing sacrificing itself for the life of another. Through the rite of fire sacrifice, fire converts the item of oblation into its spiritual essence by destroying its physical form. This essence rises in the form of smoke where it can reach the abode of the gods, who receive and accept the gifts passed to them by the fire. A gift requires a gift, and the blessings of the gods travel through door that has been created through the fire and through the recitation of prayers and holy names during the sacrifice. Alternately, when meat is boiled over a sacrificial fire, it transforms it from something mundane into something holy, and the blessings of the gods are consumed by the community. While an examination of Loki's mythos and symbolism could offer a devotee many different ways in which to perform a ceremony such as this, this is one example.

What you will need:
A fire pit or fireplace
Birch wood or twigs
A lighter or strike-a-light
Lokean recels
Your blót bowl
Something to sacrifice.

This might include some kind of hard alcohol or mead, a plate of herbs or flowers, meat, hearts (beef or chicken can be found in some stores), grains, or fruits. I recommend you think of this sacrifice as an exchange and think symbolically. Offer things that symbolically represent blessings you would like to receive in your own life. If you're trying to burn larger sacrifices like hearts or fruits, you will need a larger, hotter fire and this should be performed outside. Smaller sacrifices are more appropriate for a fireplace.

To begin, use your Lokean recels and cleansing ceremony to purify the space you will be performing your ritual in. Next, arrange the wood in your fire pit or fireplace. I recommend using birch wood as part of your kindling, as it is specifically symbolic of Laufey: Loki's mother. Birch was also considered to be a holy, healing tree in Northern Europe. You can either light your fire with modern methods, or you can use a strike-a-light method to represent a lightning strike and Loki's father Fárbauti. After you have lit your fire, say a prayer inviting Loki to the ritual space, such as:

Loki, Lord of heaven's fire
Lightning swift Loptr, come
Greet me kindly Gammleið
Great priest of sacrifices
Fill my heart with your flames
First among Muspell's sons

Cunning one, roaring one
Carry my prayers
Across the Ása Bridge
Through you the gods receive their gifts
May they ever grow in might
Mighty king, clothed in red and gold
May there ever be frith between us
Hail Loki

Keep feeding the fire until it's hot enough to place your offerings in it. When you're ready, pour a libation of your choice into your blót bowl and hold it over the fire. Say a prayer of oblation to Sigyn (something like the one that you learned in chapter 8 is a good choice):

Sig, sig, sig
Sigyn grants sure victory
To worthy gods and men
Through your hands pour all oblations
Bring our blessed offerings
To the bright burden of your arms
Gateway through which the gods
Gladly feast and grow in strength
Gift for gift, may be ever gain
The grace of our elder Kin.
Hail Loki, Hail Sigyn.

When you've finished your prayer, pour a little bit of the libation into the fire, then drink some yourself. If you're performing this blót in a group, pass the bowl to everyone present and let them drink some of the offering too. Any leftovers should be poured into the fire. When this first offering is complete, you can start to put other offerings you've prepared into the fire. Each time you put something in, accompany it with either a prayer of praise to

Loki, a personal petition, or if you aren't sure what to say, use the chant you learned in chapter 5:

Heill ver þú nú, Loki (Hail ver thoo noo, Loki)

When all of the offerings have been burned, you can either allow the fire to burn out on its own while you continue your ritual with divination, personal cleansing, meditation, or anything else you desire, or you can put the fire out. Before putting the fire out, say a final thank you and farewell to Loki and Sigyn. Though this example was a devotional for Loki, the same model can be used to give burnt offerings to any of the gods. All you would need to do to tailor this to another deity is choose appropriate offerings for them, and offer invocations and prayers to them as you're putting their offerings into the fire.

Chapter 11

Becoming a Lokean

In Icelandic literature, we sometimes come across the word *fulltrúi* ("one in whom you put your full confidence") to describe the relationship certain people held with one god in particular. This is similar to the concept of a patron or matron deity, where a worshipper feels a special bond with a specific god and makes the worship of that deity the center of their own spiritual practice. While there didn't seem to be any specific ritual involved in claiming a *fulltrúi* in Pagan Scandinavia, many modern Heathens have adopted the idea of "oathing" or "pledging" themselves to a god's service in a more ritualistic fashion. The Icelandic text *Landnámabók* contains an example of oaths being sworn on a ring, invoking Freyr and Njörðr in particular to witness the oath. Making oaths seems to have been serious business, as the oath-taker invoked curses upon themselves if they broke the oath and were considered to be outcasts in the community if the broken oath was severe enough[34].

I have often heard people ask if there is any kind of ritual or initiation that needs to take place to become a Lokean. Strictly speaking, the only thing required to be a Lokean is to worship Loki as either your *fulltrúi* or as a deity that holds a significant place in your life. There is no Lokean hierarchy and no organized lineage to pass on, and you can be a Lokean whether you identify as a Heathen, a Pagan, a Witch, a Polytheist, or something else entirely. However, I also understand the desire and need to create an exterior expression of an inner reality, especially if you want to perform a devotional gesture to formally acknowledge Loki's place in your heart or life. For those people who have developed a strong devotional relationship with Loki and want to claim him as their *fulltrúi*, I'm including a ritual of my own making by which you can "initiate" yourself into walking the road of a Lokean. This ritual doesn't carry any kind of official legitimacy, but will carry as much weight as you and Loki choose to give it.

Making an oath or ritual gesture such as this isn't a step that should be taken lightly, as once you have called the power of a god into your life it's not a simple matter of returning it for a refund if things don't work out. Answering the call of a deity such as Loki puts them in a special position where they become your partner and teacher for life. The closest equivalency I can think of to explain the *fulltrúi* relationship is that of a husband or wife versus just a friendly acquaintance: you are choosing the person who will know you most intimately, who you will prioritize, who you will dedicate the most work to building a relationship with, whose council you will seek for any important choices, and who you will seek to know and understand. This isn't a choice that should be made lightly, and there's no reason to jump into this kind of relationship while you are still getting to know Loki. I therefore wouldn't perform this ritual just for fun or as an experiment. But if and when you are ready, I offer it to you as a way to honor Loki's place in your spiritual life.

While there is no particular Lokean "code" that must be followed in order to be authentic, I'm including a list of Lokean "virtues" that I created as an alternative to the "9 Noble Virtues" espoused by certain members of the Heathen community. These are virtues that I have personally found to be relevant to Loki and walking his path, and they might serve as a meditation tool for those who feel drawn to worshipping him as a major part of their spiritual lives.

Nine Lokean Virtues

1. **Truth:** Be real. Be true to yourself and allow others to follow their own truth.
2. **Humor:** Learn to find the humor in things, especially in yourself.

3. **Humility:** If you need to tie your balls to a goat to accomplish your goals, suck it up buttercup.
4. **Cunning:** Try to think outside the box. Don't make a mess so big that you can't figure your way out of it.
5. **Transformation:** Don't be afraid of change, because that's how we grow. Don't be afraid of self-examination and listen to constructive criticism.
6. **Creativity:** Create awesome stuff. Try new things out. If you don't like it, blow it up and try again.
7. **Accountability:** You are the only one in charge of your own destiny, your own life, and your own actions.
8. **Empathy:** Try to see things from more than one perspective. Shape-shift into someone else's shoes before you pass judgement.
9. **Experimentation:** A mistake is only a mistake if you do it twice. Until then, everything is an experiment.

A Lokean Dedication Ritual

Keep in mind, just performing this dedication and saying you're a Lokean isn't what will make you one. A Lokean is something you become by walking with Loki in your day to day life and doing the work.

What you will need:
A fire pit or fireplace
Birch wood or twigs
A lighter or strike-a-light
Lokean recels
Loki oil
Your Snaptun Stone image
Your blót bowl
A libation of your choice
1 Lancet
Some kind of token to represent your commitment. This can

be a ring, and arm-ring, a pendant of some kind, a stone heart, or even the Logaþore amulet you created. This is completely up to you.

Either a cloth heart that you have sewn yourself, or a real heart bought form a butcher. If you choose to make a cloth heart, you can fill it with herbs, words of devotion written on paper, or anything else you find significant to Loki and want to include as an offering.

This is a ritual performed best outside with a fire pit, and ideally in a place that holds special significance to you. If you can perform it at night under the light of Lokabrenna, all the better. Near where your ritual fire will be, build a small altar to Loki. On it, include your Loki candle, your recels, your blót bowl, your Snaptun Stone image, your token, your Loki oil, your heart offering, your lancet, and the libation you'll be offering.

Cleanse the space with your Loki candle and recels in the usual way before lighting your ritual fire. As I stated before, using birch wood in your kindling and a strike-a-light method to light your fire holds symbolic and spiritual significance, but do what you are able to. What's most important is that the fire gets lit. When the fire is going, bow to the fire slightly and say your candle prayer:

I light the flame of Loki, both without me and within me

Take a few moments to practice your fire breathing. As you feel the light of Loki's flames filling your body, take a moment to reach out with your heart and feel his energy: ecstatic, wild, hot, fierce, lusty, angry, however it comes. When you feel that connection, speak to the fire and call him with words like:

Loki, Loðúrr, Loptr, I call you!
Logaþore, Roaring One, Trickster, I call you!

Sigyn's Burden, Scar Lipped, Bound God I call you!
I call you forth from the Kettle-grove
To join me in the place of sacrifice
By blood, by bone, by flame, I call you!
Hail Loki!

When you feel Loki's presence and are ready to continue, pick up the heart you will be offering him. Take a moment to hold it and pour your desire and devotion into it. Whisper spontaneous words of love into it or sit in meditative silence. Imagine that the heart in your hand isn't just an object: as you hold it, visualize it transforming into your own heart. When this visualization is strong, speak something to the effect of:

Cunning God, Consumer of Hearts
I offer mine to you on a burning pyre
Burn away all obstacles to you
Consume my refuse, Vulture God
And leave me as pure bones
I offer my heart as a living shrine
A temple to your holy flame
May you be my guiding torch, Fire from Heaven
As I walk the road of your mysteries.
Walk with me in life, Lóðurr
Walk with me until death, Gammleið
And towards whatever lies beyond.
Loki Laufeyjarson, I give my heart to you

When you're ready, throw the heart into the flames. Watch it burn, and know that Loki is accepting your offering. Feel the heart in your chest fill with the red flames of devotion: burning hotter and hotter as your offering burns.

When you feel ready to continue, pour your libation into your blót bowl and use your lancet on your finger to add a drop or two of your blood. Hold your bowl over the fire, imagining that the libation is being filled with the might of Loki's flames. As you hold the bowl, you might quietly chant the word *sigr* ("victory") in honor of Sigyn. When you're ready, say something to the effect of:

> By this drink may we ever be bound by blood and fire.

Take a small sip of the libation before pouring some into the fire: not so much as to put the fire out. This drink seals your oath. When you're ready, put the bowl aside and pick up your token. Hold it over the fire and imagine it filling with Loki's might. When this visualization is strong, say something to the effect of:

> By this_____ I name you my fulltrúi: my fully trusted one.

Either put on your token or set it aside. When you're ready, pick up your Loki oil. Anoint yourself with the oil, making the sign of Kenaz on your hands, head, heart, crown and token if you wish. Say something to the effect of:

> Net Weaver, Spider, Spinner of Wyrd
> May all Gods and Norns witness
> That I anoint myself as your kin
> Hail Loki!

When your ritual is complete, you can conclude it however you wish. If you use any divination techniques, you might do a reading to gain insight into your new (or renewed) road as a Lokean. You can also pray, talk to Loki, or engage in any devotional activity of your choice.

Know that going forward you have made a lifelong pledge of devotion to Loki, but that doesn't mean the work is over.

Devotion is not always easy thing, as Sigyn will tell you. Down the road, you might feel bored or burnt out. Your arms might get tired sometimes, and you may not feel like holding the bowl of devotion anymore. Know that sometimes our devotion will be tested. But just like Sigyn, we don't drop the bowl just because we don't feel like holding it anymore and we don't abandon our gods when they become inconvenient. Sigyn is here to teach us that only through love can we find the strength and the will to hold the bowl.

A Lokean Daily Practice

The rituals you've learned in this book form a basic, functional blueprint for a Lokean devotional practice. For those who might be interested in engaging in a daily devotional practice to Loki, this is a simple model that you can follow to get started. A daily practice is a portion of time you set aside (however much or little is up to you) in order to honor the gods, check in with yourself, and spend some time refilling your spiritual cup. As someone who has been keeping a (more or less) daily spiritual practice for many years, I would say to do what you can to keep this an enjoyable experience for yourself. You don't necessarily need to be up at 5 AM in meditation with Loki for an hour every day to be a "serious" devotee. A daily practice should never become guilt-ridden drudgery. Even spending five minutes a day with Loki and remembering to keep him in your thoughts during your daily life is a worthy a devotional act.

The only strict guideline that I recommend is to hold your daily practice in the same place every day: ideally this will be at a permanent alter space that you keep for Loki in your home. It doesn't matter how big or small the shrine is, but in my experience, places where prayer and devotion occur regularly begin to take on a holiness of their own.

What to Keep on Your Altar:

Your Loki candle
Your Snaptun Stone image
Loki recels
Loki oil
Your blót bowl
Loki prayer beads

Putting It All Together:

1. Light your Loki Candle, bow slightly to it, and say the candle prayer. (Ch. 1)

2. Practice your fire breathing. (Ch. 1)

3. Burn your Lokean recels, say the cleansing prayer, use them to cleanse yourself and your prayer space. (Ch. 2)

4. Anoint yourself with your Loki Oil and perform the Sovereignty Blessing (Ch. 9)

5. Pour a libation into your blót bowl as an offering to Loki. Say the Sigyn Prayer, charge the offering with the fire breath, and take a sip. (Ch. 8)

6. Use your Loki Prayer Beads and a prayer or chant of your choice to help you enter into a prayerful, meditative state. (Ch. 5)

7. Spend the rest of your time with Loki in any way you wish. You can talk to him, do divination, read stories or books about him, journal, make art, whatever your heart desires. In my experience, mixing things up now and then is a way to ensure that your devotional practice doesn't become boring or stale. Keep yourself motivated with new practices you want to explore and things you want to learn.

Conclusion

"I am the mother of Odin's stallion, Sleipnir. I am the father of Fenrir Sun-Eater, and of Hel Half-Rotted and of Jormungand the World-Serpent. I am Loki Scar-Lip, Loki Skywalker, Loki Gaint's Child, Loki Lie-Smith. I am Loki, who is fire and wit and hate. I am Loki. And I will be under an obligation to no one." - Neil Gaiman, *The Kindly Ones*

I hope that you've enjoyed this introduction to Loki and his mysteries. This book represents only some of the ways in which one devotee has experienced and interpreted him. As this trickster and shapeshifter wears many masks, the ways in which he can be encountered are undoubtedly limitless.

There are those who would say that Loki is bound under the earth to this day: waiting in limbo until the world finally meets its inevitable end. I don't see Ragnarök as a distant event, far off in the future as much as I see it as a continuous cycle of deaths and rebirths in our lives. We will all go through many "Ragnaröks", endings and transformations from one phase of life into another. As long as our unpredictable world is still moving and changing, Loki's influence and power is present. You can hear his laughter in the crackling flame and the flash of lightning. He is in every chance encounter, every burst of gleeful inspiration, every happy accident, and every act of disobedience. Whether you love him or revile him, worship him or snub him, Loki is alive and well in our world.

Now and forever, Hail Loki!

Endnotes

1. Sturluson, Snorri and Faulkes, Anthony. *Edda*. Everyman, 1995. 26
2. Turville-Petre, E.O.G. *Myth and Religion of the North: The Religion of Ancient Scandinavia*. Greenwood, 1975. 126
3. Ibid.141
4. Rooth, Anna Birgitta, *Loki in Scandinavian Mythology*. C.W.K. Gleerups Förlag, Lund, 1961
5. Thorsson, Edred, Rune-Song. *Runa-Raven Press*. 1993. 23
6. Simek, Rudolf, *Dictionary of Northern Mythology*. D.S Brewer, 2007. 198
7. Simek, Rudolf, *Dictionary of Northern Mythology*. D.S Brewer, 2007. 355
8. Þorgilsson, Ari, Ellwood, Thomas. The Book of the Settlement of Iceland. T. Wilson, 1898. 194
9. Olrik, Axel and Eli, Anker. Loke in the Younger Tradition. Northvegr.org, 2004-2007. http://jillian.rootaction.net/~jill ian/world_faiths/www.northvegr.org/lore/olrik002/ titlepage.html
10. Simek, Rudolf, *Dictionary of Northern Mythology*. D.S Brewer, 2007. 195
11. Author's translation
12. Þorgeirsson, Haukur. Kokkur, *Lóðurr and Late Evidence*. RMN Newsletter, May 2011, No. 2. (Folklore Studies/Dept. Of Philosophy, History, Culture, and Art Studies, University of Helsinki, Helsinki.
13. MacLeod, Mindy, and Bernhard Mees. *Runic Amulets and Magic Objects*. Boydell Press, 2014. 17-18
14. Tacitus and Birley, Anthony, *Agricola and Germany*. OUP Oxford, 1999. 47
15. Amatørarkæolog finder Odin-amulet - eller er det Loke?, Mynewsdesk, 7 Sept. 2015, http://www.mynewsdesk.com/

dk/pressreleases/amatoerarkaeolog-finder-odin-amulet-eller-er-det-loke-1212729

16. Turville-Petre, E.O.G. *Myth and Religion of the North: The Religion of Ancient Scandinavia.* Greenwood, 1975. 186

17. Sturluson, Snorri. *Edda.* Trans. Anthony Faulkes. London: Dent, 1995. 154

18. Lindow, John. *Norse Mythology: A Guide to Gods, Heroes, Rituals, and Beliefs.* Oxford University Press, 2002. 269

19. Cleasby, Richard. *An Icelandic-English Dictionary.* Oxford University Press, 1957. 79

20. Winroth, Anders, Al-Tartushi on Hedeby. Yale, 2006. https:// classesv2.yale.edu/access/content/user/haw6/Vikings/al-Tartushi.html

21. Hesiod, and West, M.L, *Theogony and Works and Days.* Oxford University Press, 2009. 18-21

22. De Vries, Jan. *The Problem of Loki.* Helenski: Suomalainen Tiedekatemia, 1933. 218

23. Rudolf, Simek. *Dictionary of Northern Mythology.* D.S Brewer, 2007. 193

24. Turville-Petre, E.O.G. Myth and Religion of the North. Greenwood Press, 1975. 131

25. Orchard, Andy, *The Elder Edda: A Book of Viking Lore.* Penguin Classics, 2011. 296

26. Simek, Rudolf, *Dictionary of Northern Mythology.* D.S Brewer, 2007. 284

27. Sturluson, Snorri and Smith, A.H. *Heimskringla: or The Lives of the Norse Kings.* Dover Publications, 1990. 87

28. Fadlan, Ibn and Flowers, Stephen E. *Ibn Fadlan's Travel-Report: As it Concerns the Scandinavian Rus.* Runa-Raven Press, 1998. 7

29. Skuggi, *Sorcerer's Screed: The Icelandic Book of Magic Spells.* Lesstofan, 2015. 58

30. Flowers, Stephen E. *The Galdrabók: An Icelandic Book of Magic.* Runa-Raven Press, 2005. 45

31. In the Elder Futhark, Kenaz means "torch". In this instance, Kenaz represents both Loki's influence as a fire deity, but also your own guiding light.
32. Davidson, H.R. Ellis. *The Road to Hel*. Greenwood Press, 1968. 9-12
33. Sturluson, Snorri and Smith, A.H. *Heimskringla or The Lives of the Norse Kings*. Dover Publications, 1990. 6-7
34. Rudolf, Simek. *Dictionary of Northern Mythology*. D.S Brewer, 2007. 238

Recommended Reading

This is a short list of works that those interested in learning more about Loki might find helpful and inspiring.

Scholarly Works
"Loke in the Younger Tradition" by Axel Olrik
"The Problem of Loki" by Jan de Vries
"Loki in Scandinavian Mythology" by Anna Birgitta Rooth
"God in Flames, God in Fetters: Loki's Role in the Northern Religions" by Stephan Grundy

Devotional Works
"Trickster, My Beloved: Poems for Laufey's Son" by Elizabeth Vongvisith
"Consuming Flame: A Devotional Anthology for Loki and His Family" by Galina Krasskova
"Worshipping Loki: A Short Introduction" by Silence Maestas
"Playing With Fire: An Exploration of Loki Laufeyjarson" by Dagulf Loptson

Fictional Works
"American Gods" by Neil Gaiman
"Odd and the Frost Giants" by Neil Gaiman
"Norse Mythology" by Neil Gaiman
"Runemarks" and "Rune Light" by Joanne M .Harris
"The Gospel of Loki" and "The Testament of Loki" by Joanne M. Harris
"Eight Days of Luke" by Diana Wynne Jones

Comparative Mythology
"Trickster Makes This World: Mischief, Myth, and Art" by Lewis Hyde

"Mythical Trickster Figures: Contours, Contexts, and Criticisms" Edited by William J Hynes and William G. Doty

"Theogony and Works and Days" by Hesiod

"Yajna: A Comprehensive Survey" by Sannyasi Gyanshruti and Sannyasi Srividyananda

"Agni: The Vedic Ritual of the Fire Altar, Vol. I and II" by Frits Staal

Bibliography

Cleasby, Richard. An Icelandic-English Dictionary. Oxford University Press, 1957

Davidson, H.R. Ellis. The Road to Hel. Greenwood Press, 1968

De Vries, Jan. The Problem of Loki. Helenski: Suomalainen Tiedekatemia, 1933

Fadlan, Ibn and Flowers, Stephen E. Ibn Fadlan's Travel-Report: As it Concerns the Scandinavian Rus. Runa-Raven Press, 1998

Flowers, Stephen E. The Galdrabók: An Icelandic Book of Magic. Runa-Raven Press, 2005

Hesiod, and West, M.L, Theogony and Works and Days. Oxford University Press, 2009

Lindow, John. Norse Mythology: A Guide to Gods, Heroes, Rituals, and Beliefs. Oxford University Press, 2002

- MacLeod, Mindy, and Bernhard Mees. Runic Amulets and Magic Objects. Boydell Press, 20 14

Olrik, Axel and Eli, Anker. Loke in the Younger Tradition. Northvegr.org, 2004-2007. http://jillian.rootaction.net/~jillian/world_faiths/www.northvegr.org/lore/olrik002/titlepage.html

Orchard, Andy, The Elder Edda: A Book of Viking Lore. Penguin Classics, 2011

Rooth, Anna Birgitta, Loki in Scandinavian Mythology. C.W.K. Gleerups Förlag, Lund, 1961

Staal, Fritz. Agni: The Vedic Ritual of the Fire Altar, Vol. 1&2, Motilal Banassidaas Publishers, 1983

Simek, Rudolf, Dictionary of Northern Mythology. D.S Brewer, 2007

Skuggi, Sorcerer's Screed: The Icelandic Book of Magic Spells. Lesstofan, 2015

Sturluson, Snorri and Faulkes, Anthony. Edda. Everyman, 1995

Sturluson, Snorri and Smith, A.H. Heimskringla: or The Lives of the Norse Kings. Dover Publications, 1990

Tacitus and Birley, Anthony, Agricola and Germany. OUP Oxford, 1999

Thorsson, Edred, Rune-Song. Runa-Raven Press. 1993

Turville-Petre, E.O.G. Myth and Religion of the North: The Religion of Ancient Scandinavia. Greenwood, 1975

Zoega, Geir T. A Concise Dictionary of Old Icelandic. University of Toronto Press, 2004

Þorgilsson, Ari, Ellwood, Thomas. The Book of the Settlement of Iceland. T. Wilson, 1898

Þorgeirsson, Haukur. Kokkur, Lóðurr and Late Evidence. RMN Newsletter, May 2011, No. 2. (Folklore Studies/Dept. Of Philosophy, History, Culture, and Art Studies, University of Helsinki, Helsinki

**MOON
BOOKS**

PAGANISM & SHAMANISM

What is Paganism? A religion, a spirituality, an alternative belief system, nature worship? You can find support for all these definitions (and many more) in dictionaries, encyclopaedias, and text books of religion, but subscribe to any one and the truth will evade you. Above all Paganism is a creative pursuit, an encounter with reality, an exploration of meaning and an expression of the soul. Druids, Heathens, Wiccans and others, all contribute their insights and literary riches to the Pagan tradition. Moon Books invites you to begin or to deepen your own encounter, right here, right now.

If you have enjoyed this book, why not tell other readers by posting a review on your preferred book site.

Recent bestsellers from Moon Books are:

Journey to the Dark Goddess
How to Return to Your Soul
Jane Meredith
Discover the powerful secrets of the Dark Goddess and
transform your depression, grief and pain into healing
and integration.
Paperback: 978-1-84694-677-6 ebook: 978-1-78099-223-5

Shamanic Reiki
Expanded Ways of Working with Universal Life Force Energy
Llyn Roberts, Robert Levy
Shamanism and Reiki are each powerful ways of healing; together,
their power multiplies. *Shamanic Reiki* introduces techniques to
help healers and Reiki practitioners tap ancient healing wisdom.
Paperback: 978-1-84694-037-8 ebook: 978-1-84694-650-9

Pagan Portals – The Awen Alone
Walking the Path of the Solitary Druid
Joanna van der Hoeven
An introductory guide for the solitary Druid, *The Awen Alone* will
accompany you as you explore, and seek out your own place
within the natural world.
Paperback: 978-1-78279-547-6 ebook: 978-1-78279-546-9

A Kitchen Witch's World of Magical Herbs & Plants
Rachel Patterson
A journey into the magical world of herbs and plants, filled with
magical uses, folklore, history and practical magic. By popular
writer, blogger and kitchen witch, Tansy Firedragon.
Paperback: 978-1-78279-621-3 ebook: 978-1-78279-620-6

Medicine for the Soul
The Complete Book of Shamanic Healing
Ross Heaven
All you will ever need to know about shamanic healing and how to
become your own shaman…
Paperback: 978-1-78099-419-2 ebook: 978-1-78099-420-8

Shaman Pathways – The Druid Shaman
Exploring the Celtic Otherworld
Danu Forest
A practical guide to Celtic shamanism with exercises and
techniques as well as traditional lore for exploring the Celtic
Otherworld.
Paperback: 978-1-78099-615-8 ebook: 978-1-78099-616-5

Traditional Witchcraft for the Woods and Forests
A Witch's Guide to the Woodland with Guided Meditations and
Pathworking
Mélusine Draco
A Witch's guide to walking alone in the woods, with guided
meditations and pathworking.
Paperback: 978-1-84694-803-9 ebook: 978-1-84694-804-6

Wild Earth, Wild Soul
A Manual for an Ecstatic Culture
Bill Pfeiffer
Imagine a nature-based culture so alive and so connected,
spreading like wildfire. This book is the first flame…
Paperback: 978-1-78099-187-0 ebook: 978-1-78099-188-7

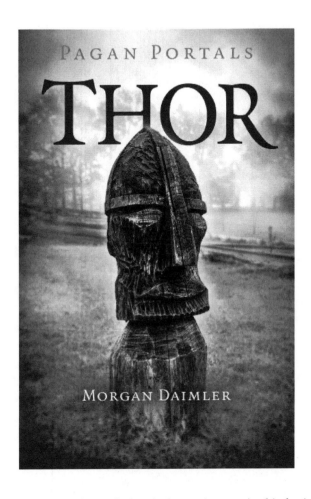

You might also like...

PAGAN PORTALS

ODIN

Meeting the Norse Allfather

MORGAN DAIMLER

...a valuable addition to any Pagan bookshelf.
Laura Perry

978-1-78535-480-9 (Paperback)
978-1-78535-481-6 (e-book)